POSITIONAL PLAY
Goalkeeping

by
Allen Wade

D0465301

Published by
REEDSWAIN INC

Library of Congress Cataloging - in - Publication Data

Wade, Allen
  Positional Play - Goalkeeping

ISBN No. 1-890946-07-9
Copyright © 1997 Allen Wade
Library of Congress Catalog Card Number 97-075740

Reedswain books are available at special discounts for bulk purchase. For details contact the Special Sales Manager at Reedswain 1-800-331-5191.

Credits: Art Direction, Layout, Design and Diagrams • Kimberly N. Bender
Cover Photo: Empics

REEDSWAIN VIDEOS AND BOOKS, INC.
612 Pughtown Road • Spring City Pennsylvania 19475
1-800-331-5191 • WWW.REEWSWAIN.COM

Table of Contents

Introduction
The Goalkeeper's Role

Within the past few years the role and the responsibilities of the soccer goalkeeper have changed enormously. The deliberate pass back to the goalkeeper, enabling him to handle the ball inside his penalty area, has been outlawed. This change has had a major effect on the game, especially on the safety play possible between backs and their goalkeeper. If change proceeds logically, any kind of back pass to a goalkeeper in his penalty area should be outlawed. Then, for the first time in the game's history, goalkeepers will have to be real soccer players in every sense of the word. And not before time!

Fifty years ago a soccer team was made up of 'specialist' players. A centre forward (today's striker) was exclusively concerned with shooting and scoring. A 'winger' specialized in running to cross the ball into the penalty area from the widest positions or he cut in from the wing to shoot. Wingers and centre forwards were required only to attack; defense was strictly for the workers.

Inside forwards (today's mid-field players) were the game's play makers. Some especially gifted players took on auxiliary scoring responsibilities. Mainly, they provided the ammunition for the centre forwards and wingers to fire the shots.

Wing half backs were also mid-field players but in those times they merely supported the inside forwards. Their roles, generally speaking, were supportive and they were the game's enforcers and often inside forwards' 'minders'.

Full-backs were exclusively committed to defending by intercepting and tackling for the ball when opposing attackers had possession. Centre half backs, in reality, were centre backs stationed between the wide full backs and exclusively concerned with defending the central zone in the air and on the ground.

Goalkeepers, of course, were there to prevent shots from going into the net and for setting the game in motion when an opposing attack broke down.

These specialist players only played in certain parts of the pitch and it was rare for interchanges of position to take place. Full-backs were opposed by wingers; centre half-backs were opposed by centre forwards; inside forwards were marked by wing half-backs and so on. Only occasionally were teams encouraged to use positional interchanges to surprise opponents.

Times have changed, most players now make much greater contributions to play. . . both in attack and defense. . . in all parts of the field. Goalkeepers today are expected to dominate certain areas and to make important contributions in many other circumstances.

Certain situations in the game are controlled by the goalkeeper and what he says to other players goes. . . and no arguments, or else!

No longer restricted to his goal area, he must be prepared to move outside the penalty area, to control and pass the ball with the confidence and security of any out-field player.

A good goalkeeper must 'read' the game as well as any good outfield player and obviously new and extended responsibilities will have important implications for the early training of goalkeepers as we shall see.

Chapter 2
The Goalkeeper's Responsibilities

2. Control.

An intelligent goalkeeper's first responsibility is to ensure that, as far as possible, he has nothing to do!

His ultimate responsibility is to save any shots at goal but this is best achieved by making as sure as he can that shots at goal do not happen.

To do so he must become one of the back-field defensive controllers.

He cannot be responsible for preventing the ball from being moved into dangerous shooting positions but he can watch for careless positioning by out-field defending players, particularly the backs, which might enable opponents to move into dangerous and perhaps unmarked positions.

A goalkeeper must become, literally, the eyes in the backs of the other players' heads!

He, better than anyone, with the exception of the centre backs perhaps, can see when opponents are being marked loosely or when they are dislocating a defense by 'pulling' their markers too far away from other defenders. The goalkeeper is the player perfectly placed to see when cover among the back defenders is poor. He, best of all defending players, can see how much time his co-defenders have. . . or don't have. . . in which to play the ball out of danger safely and securely. It is his responsibility to set up effective lines of communication so that safe play under pressure is assured.

2.2 Communication.

When outfield players are under threat from opponents, the goalkeeper is perfectly positioned to tell them exactly what is happening. And they really do need to know! He is one of the important integrating influences in defensive play.

Without direction, without defensive co-ordination, defenders may be tempted to play for themselves and in so doing become dangerous players. . . to their own team!

2.3 Safety.

The goalkeeper's third responsibility is to move outside his penalty area to act as a second 'sweeper' whenever opponents attempt to play long passes behind his backs or when his backs are under pressure facing their own goal and need a safe outlet. These situations usually occur when the goalkeeper's team has been drawn well forward in attack so that the backs are close to the half way line. Opponents may try to draw the central backs to one side of the field before switching the point of attack in the opposite direction. Diagram 1.

Alert goalkeepers, with competent trapping, controlling and kicking. . . and even heading. . . techniques, can cut out these dangerous 'switch play' moves.

Modern goalkeepers need specially designed functional practices in which to develop the perception and the skills of out-field players.

Simple one-to-one, throw and catch, handling and diving practices, which make up the bulk of so-called goalkeeper coaching and practice situations, are not enough.

Later, we shall see how goalkeepers' functional practices are designed and used to develop their perceptual and conceptual skills.

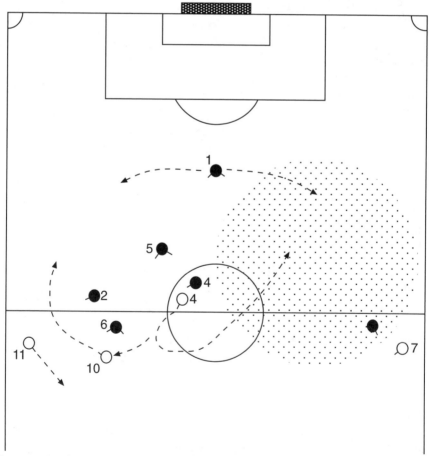

Diagram 1. *The goalkeeper as auxiliary sweeper covered threatened space.*

Regular practice as a sweeper, or in any of the back defenders' positions, whether a team plays with a sweeper or not, provides invaluable experience for a goalkeeper.

2.4 Command

The next responsibility is for the goalkeeper to command, physically, as much of the penalty area as he can. He must accept personal responsibility for challenging and for gaining possession of the ball whenever it is moved into the penalty area, provided that he can do so with a significant chance of success.

This will involve moving off his goal line to catch or punch the ball whenever it is transferred into the penalty area. The greater the area which he seeks to command, the better his anticipation, his speed off the mark and his jumping and catching abilities must be.

Whenever an opponent seems about to shoot, it is the goalkeeper's responsibility to move out to put the opponent under pressure by attacking the ball while presenting the largest possible barrier to the shot.

These skills rarely find places in the training and practice routines of goalkeepers because few coaches have the necessary insight into the goalkeeper's special problems or the ingenuity to create relevant and realistic practices.

Gaining clean and undisputed possession of the ball in all circumstances where he is able to do so SAFELY is, in many respects, the true hallmark of the great 'keeper. To catch the ball his positioning must be radar-like in its precision. High class positional play makes goalkeeping look easy and unspectacular. Some goalkeepers, even some international goalkeepers . . . usually bad ones. . . work very hard at making goalkeeping look difficult. Deliberately late jumps and dives followed by one handed punches or deflections make goalkeeping look hair raisingly spectacular. To people who know better, what seems to be hair-raising to the spectator is stomach-sinking for the coach!

Spectacular goalkeeping usually is achieved only at the expense of safety.

There is nothing more demoralizing for an attack to face a goalkeeper who seems to catch everything while barely stretching for the ball.

When gaining possession of the ball safely seems doubtful, it is the responsibility of the goalkeeper to see that the ball is deflected out of play or into a totally safe area.

2.5 Confidence.

The goalkeeper's next responsibility is for establishing and maintaining calmness and confidence throughout his team. He has the enormous advantage of being able to use his hands to bring play to a halt. In possession of the ball, he controls everything and he must employ that advantage with such massive authority that it seems to be almost unfair. And he has no need to be noisy about it!

In English professional soccer there is a belief. . . totally mistaken. . . that all players should shout at each other all the time. The belief is that shouting:

(a) encourages those on the receiving end and
(b) is needed by players who are concentrating on playing the ball.
Neither is true.

For a player about to use a difficult skill under extreme pressure there are few things he wants less than other players screaming instructions or exhorting him to 'watch out' for this or that.

When it is the goalkeeper shouting, in and near to the penalty area, it is downright unnerving.

Calling for the ball positively and confidently is important in enabling co-defenders to benefit from the goalkeeper's advantages.

Communication between players is important in developing a better understanding of what each player's capabilities in any particular situation are. Indiscriminate shouting at other players can and often does destroy confidence.

Telling a teammate what to do, all the time, implies that he doesn't know what to do and that you do! Most soccer players worth the name might find that mildly. . . or not so mildly insulting.

Inform players by all means, advise them when necessary but do it calmly and confidently and they will play calmly and confidently. Scream and shout anxiously or angrily and the players who are shouted at will play anxiously and fearfully.

Inevitably, they will make mistakes but then mistakes are inevitable in all parts of the field.

2.6 Construction.

The fifth and the goalkeeper's remaining responsibilities are concerned with attacking play.

Safety first, second and last are a goalkeeper's watchwords. Nevertheless, while he is best placed to appreciate the problems faced by defenders, he is also best placed to see the possibilities for counter attack if he develops the perception (vision) to assess possibilities as soon as they occur. . . if not sooner! His vision will only improve if he trains himself to read the whole action picture all of the time, not merely the immediate action picture some of the time or when it is near to him.

Those areas of the pitch most remote from the immediate action are often those most readily available for counter attack.

The delivery of the ball, thrown or kicked by the goalkeeper, must pose no controlling problems for the receiving player.

Any threat of interception or of an opponent moving to tackle, means that the goalkeeper must change his mind. . . quickly.

A reasonable rule for a goalkeeper in possession of the ball is that if he has to change his mind, he should change it again.

This ensures that he has time to consider and even reconsider his pass options. Occasionally the state of a match demands that everyone's play is speeded up: when a team is losing 1-0 say with five minutes left on the clock. Even so, it's better to be one goal behind with one minute to play than to go two goals behind as a result of taking risks to get the ball into play hurriedly and thereby inaccurately.

When passing to mount a counter attack, the ball must be thrown or kicked close to the receiving player's feet unless there is a considerable distance between him and the nearest opponent. How far is considerable? It depends upon the distances between the goalkeeper and the target player, the target player and the nearest defender and how quickly and safely the ball can be dispatched to the target player.

The longer the throw out (or kick) the more time a defender will have to move into a challenging position while the ball is in the air.

2.7 Clearance.

As his team moves out into counter attack it is the responsibility of the goalkeeper to make sure that back defenders push forward to leave as much space as possible between themselves and the goalkeeper. If they push forward compactly and positively they force their opponents to move away from goal in order to stay 'on-side'. This gives a goalkeeper plenty of space. . . and therefore time. . . in which to re-assess playing developments.

Confusion occurs when backs fail to clear space in front of their goalkeeper by moving out behind their attack too slowly. One of the backs . . . preferably the sweeper if a team plays with one. . . should drive the other players up-field but even an experienced sweeper benefits from an extra pair of eyes behind him. That extra pair of eyes is the goalkeeper's.

2.8 Shot Stopping.

First and last the goalkeeper is responsible for stopping shots.

He must position himself so that he always has the clearest possible sight of the ball whoever has it and whoever is about to receive it.

He must anticipate the intentions of all attackers preferably before they even have the ball.

He must read shooting situations almost as well as attackers themselves;

some goalkeepers read them better!

Peter Shilton, a vastly experienced, world rated, England international goalkeeper, was infinitely better at selling dummies to attackers than they were at selling dummies to him.

Here again there are important implications for the type of practice best suited to the goalkeeper's needs.

Unfortunately, while the goalkeeper's responsibilities have changed and multiplied, the coaching and training of goalkeepers has remained in the Stone Age.

Those then are the seven commandments for effective goalkeeping. They are learned only by repeated experience and by concentrated study of the soccer situations in which they occur; in other words through realistic and controlled practice.

Chapter 3
The Main Attributes
of a Goalkeeper

'Goalkeepers are born not made' said someone who couldn't have been more wrong. Goalkeepers in common with all soccer players learn to play at very early ages. Certainly the exceptional ones make a commitment to the position quite early in life because they find they are good at it. They sense that they have the right attributes even though at that early age they probably couldn't spell the word, let alone define it.

'El Tel' Venables, former England coach, is reported as offering the opinion that goalkeepers aren't real soccer players, they are only ball handlers.

He is probably right but he should not be. In the next few years greater demands will be made for all round soccer competence in goalkeepers than was ever envisaged by the game's founders a hundred and more years ago. Changes in the laws of the game recently enacted and more changes to come will require goalkeepers to have significantly increased attributes.

3.1 Play Reading.

Goalkeepers must become first rate readers of game flow and movement patterns development. This means that they need to be students of the game and to develop a general game sense, a 'feeling' for what is likely to happen in any given circumstance. In any case they have long periods during match play when they couldn't spend their time better. It's one thing to look at what is going on however, and quite another to know how to look at a game. Goalkeepers need to be taught what to look for and, for that matter, so do most other players: few are.

The best way for a goalkeeper to develop game sense is to take every opportunity to practice in outfield positions, particularly in the back positions, not forgetting time necessary for development as a goalkeeper of course.

Most spectators, excited by the game, only see the action close to the ball. To develop a sense of the game, a player needs to watch the movements and the physical 'attitudes' of players quite remote from immediate action areas.

How do players stand and move when not involved in play? What do they seem to be thinking about. To what extent, if at all, do they adjust their positions to play when the likelihood of their involvement in it in the foreseeable future is remote? Are they absorbed in play or mentally removed from it? Do they only come alive when immediate action threatens? Do they remain in defensive positions or do they seek to get involved in all phases of play?

In addition, when a goal threat occurs, an observer needs to be able to re-run preceding actions in his mind to trace the source of such errors as may have occurred leading up to danger in a key area.

Sometimes one player makes an obvious error for which a team is punished; quite often that player is likely to be the goalkeeper. It is one thing to apportion blame to the obvious player, it is quite another to identify general technical or tactical deficiencies which contributed to the ultimate mistake. Pinning the blame for errors on any single player is unwise and unprofitable.

'All for one and one for all' as eleven musketeers would have said if they had been a soccer team.

3.2 Concentration.
Reading play, the study of actions far removed from the goalkeeper's home territory, involves long periods of concentration. Goalkeepers should focus their attention on play to such an extent that the existence of spectators and other 'outsiders' is lost completely.

Concentration is a learned skill although some players adapt to it more quickly and easily than others. It involves high levels of perseverance.

My own experience, for what it's worth, told me that concentration was improved when I focused my attention first on one player, opponent or team mate, to categorize and mentally record such skill strengths and deficiencies as I could identify. Then I moved on to mentally recording repeated co-operation moves between players, ours or theirs. Certain players in most teams unconsciously or consciously seek out tactical relationships with other players; they enjoy collaborating. Even when a move fails, both players take some pleasure from having tried it. This kind of inter-play often becomes a dominant consideration in analyzing a team's play and tactics.

Players who are friends off the field will look for opportunities to cement such friendships on it.

Some players go to considerable lengths to try to break an opponent's concentration. They joke with him: make comments about his team mates to him: cast doubts about his parentage: claim dissatisfaction with their current employers and inquire about a possible transfer and so on. The 'try-ons' are limitless but they show how important highly focused concentration is to other players.
They know you know!

3.3 Will Power.

I was tempted to write 'courage' but on reflection preferred the more general term. Good goalkeepers are brave but in a calculated way. They see the need for certain actions and have the determination i.e. the will power, to see them through. The consequences of what they are about to do other than success in execution rarely enters their heads. I say rarely because with experience comes a greater awareness of the personal consequences of certain dangerous acts. Young goalkeepers, unaware perhaps of just how serious the dangers of a certain action can be, simply do it.

They are fearless because they have no experience upon which to be fearful.

With experience a goalkeeper learns how to take on dangerous actions having calculated the consequences but knowing, through experience, how to minimize personal danger.

Experience may cause a goalkeeper to choose an option which minimizes the danger to him but which, without the calculation involved, might have made an action more dangerous but also more likely to have been successful. Experience has its price.

To overcome known dangers and problems a player must become very determined; he must develop exceptional will power, the capacity for overcoming problems and obstructions of all kinds. There are simple exercises which help in the development of this attribute but they are not within the scope of this book.

3.4 Decisiveness.

Again I was tempted, tempted to write 'aggression' but on further reflection I concluded that aggression may imply a certain overwhelming effort or commitment and even lack of control. An exceptional soccer player must be decisive; he must program all the relevant options and make accurate judgments before acting. Of course reading that, as set down here, there is an implication of time needed and taken to come to decisions. In fact decisiveness in a game like soccer is based upon an enormous mental library of knowledge, understanding and general experience as a result of which so much information is processed without conscious thought and very quickly.

Those aspects of the process of arriving at decisive action which do take time are those which are new, probably, to a player's library of experience.

Nevertheless a goalkeeper, whatever his level of experience, must be decisive for the very important reason that his co-defenders rely heavily on him for certainty of action in many situations.

It is better for a goalkeeper to be decisive and wrong than not decisive at all. We all learn from our mistakes, goalkeepers more than most.

3.5 Confidence.

True confidence comes from an inner knowledge and certainty of one's capabilities plus a willingness to extend those capabilities.

Goalkeepers may occasionally feel as apprehensive about certain soccer situations as other players; they will not show it.

Goalkeepers, along with central backs, are the best positioned of all soccer players to show and spread confidence. Confidence is what you feel and also what you show. A player may feel apprehensive but will not show it. At the same time what may be a highly, overt show of super confidence or superiority may in fact be a demonstration of an inferiority complex. Most outfield players are much more impressed by quiet assuredness, with the goalkeeper expressing general encouragement quietly and without any sign of anxiety, than with noisy exhortations.

In recent years goalkeepers shouting at the tops of their voices in all phases of play have become commonplace. These sort of extravagances may appeal to the crowd or look good on TV but they will do little for the confidence of other players.

Goalkeepers should be seen but rarely heard.

The first five goalkeeper attributes stated previously are what might be described as mental or psychological.

The next are, broadly speaking, physical.

3.6 Agility.

Soccer agility is the ability to change position on the ground or through the air and to change the shape of the body, often at high speed.

In addition, goalkeeper agility involves catching, punching, deflecting kicking or throwing the ball, all of this at optimum speed while impeded or challenged by one or more players.

A goalkeeper must run in all directions often at high speed while preparing to jump off either or both feet into a ground or aerial dive. These are gymnastic rather than athletic actions.

3.7 Speed.

A goalkeeper must be fast in all bodily (limb) movements when required. There are different forms of speed.

First there is action speed, speed of bodily or limb movement, the sort of speed fundamental to improving agility for example.

Second there is reaction speed, the speed needed to act when a player has had little or no time to judge and decide what action to take.

Finally there is anticipation speed, the speed developed out of a deep understanding of players' probable actions in different situations and the speed needed to take advantage of that insight.

The last quality is by far the most important; highly developed it can almost eliminate the need for the first two qualities. I did say almost!

Players are born with neuro-physiological advantages or disadvantages.

Pure reaction time may be a genetic factor in human performance. Speed of muscular contraction, also, may be genetically influenced to a significant extent. We can do little about our genes but we can compensate for deficiencies, we can improve movement speed through specifically designed, scientifically based exercise programs.

Anticipation speed is a skill. It can be improved far more than either action or reaction speed through practice and training. We are not born with skills, they are learned through insight and progressive, specific practice.

3.8 Power.

Goalkeepers need power if by power you mean what I mean. Power, in the context of soccer, is a product of strength and speed.

The quality needed to propel 180 lbs of flesh and bone say, over several yards at maximum speed is power. The quality needed to run and jump to optimum height while obstructed by one or more human bodies is power.

The word power induces an idea of bulk; powerful men are visualized as big men. This is not necessarily the case. Many big men are not powerful and cannot generate the speed and strength of muscular contraction to put their bulk into action.

For goalkeepers, size, i.e. height, can be an advantage but many relatively short goalkeepers have been outstandingly successful if they have been powerfully agile. Indeed excessive height can be a disadvantage if it reduces a player's speed of action or reaction.

The need for goalkeepers to overcome physical challenge from other players is important; doing so requires a player to be powerful.

3.9 Suppleness.

The gymnastic requirements of goalkeepers place great stress on their limbs and particularly on those complexes of muscles, ligaments and tendons which make up and surround their joints. Action response times limited to almost zero mean that the relationship between any limb and another part of the body occasionally may be stretched beyond the normal. . . well beyond it. These are classic conditions for tendon and ligament tears and ruptures. It follows that goalkeepers who are very supple are less likely to suffer injuries of these kinds.

Suppleness is best achieved through specific, regular, exercise routines started at an early age and maintained throughout life.

The joint complexes most at risk in goalkeeping are:

- the neck and shoulders
- the back (especially the lower back)
- the hips
- the arms and hands, particularly the last.

A stiff goalkeeper is a handicapped goalkeeper.

The attributes listed would I am sure be found in my ideal goalkeeper. Using a score range of one to ten for each attribute, very few if any goalkeepers would score all tens. Perfection is an ideal, not a realistic proposition. Nevertheless, this list of attributes, or others if you wish, is a useful basis upon which to assess goalkeeping potential.

From time to time there will emerge small, spindly players who look as though they might benefit from a good meal and who look as though they might not be with us for long in a strong wind but who are outstanding at getting the ball and stopping shots. Good luck to them.

Chapter 4
Goalkeeping Tactics

I t will be obvious that the previously stated responsibilities have important implications for the group tactics which a goalkeeper and his co-
defenders will develop to gain advantage in different situations.

The primary purpose of group tactics is to make the best possible use of
the personal capabilities of each player while hiding, as far as possible, any
weaknesses.

The secondary purpose is to exploit any weakness evident among
opposing players while limiting their ability to capitalize on their
strengths.

All players develop their own individual, tactical skills. Many of these
skills may seem to have little or nothing to do with the actual playing of
the game of soccer. A great many are almost entirely psychological and
could be used in any competitive game. They are very important.

Some experts consider that mastery of these personal tactical skills is the
difference between ordinary and outstanding players. I certainly do!

4.1 Cover and Balance.

Good defenders cover each other whenever there is the likelihood of an
opponent attacking one of their number in a dangerous part of the field.
The primary danger areas are the shooting zones; those areas from which
shots on goal are most likely to score. In diagram 2, they have the low
numbers. The cross hatched shaded areas are the areas from which most
goals are scored and from which the most dangerous deliveries are made.

The goalkeeper is ideally positioned to see when and where the danger
areas are poorly defended and covered and which opponents are most
likely to pose the greatest threats to security in those areas. .

In diagram 3, the attacker black 10 is making a positive run at goal with
the ball. If he can penetrate the shaded area behind white 6, the defending team is in trouble. The sweeper centre back, white 5, has not moved
over far enough to cover the space behind white 6.

His goalkeeper must tell him to do so. . . decisively and quickly.

When that has been done, the goalkeeper will look to see if white 3,
who is best positioned to give the ultimate cover, has also moved over.

Any sudden switch of play in the direction of black 11 can be covered
by white 2 but the threat of a central breakthrough will have been
stopped and the defense is again well balanced because of white 3's move
towards centre field at the back.

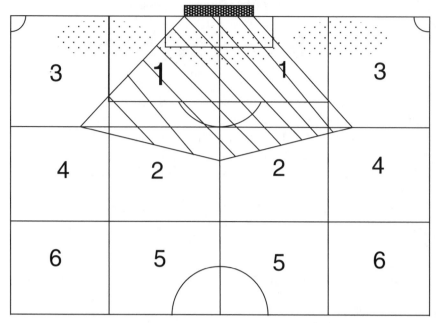

Diagram 2. *The lower the number the higher its priority in defense. Cross hatch areas are especially important.*

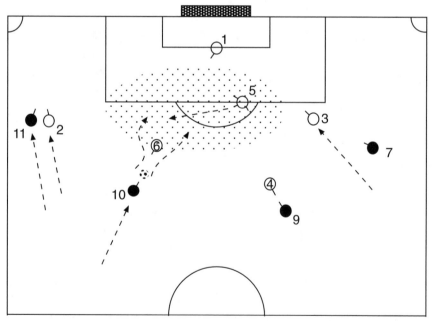

Diagram 3. *The goalkeeper as a back-field controller.*

These covering and balancing moves take place quickly when a team is defending in its back third of the pitch.

Defenders occasionally become lazy or lose their concentration or they become over concerned with the movement of a nearby opposing player so that they 'forget' their responsibilities for collective defense. It's the goalkeeper's job to stay alert and watch out for these mental blackouts. He, after all, pays the final price for everyone else's mistakes!

In diagram 4, where play is developing against his right defensive flank, the goalkeeper has noticed the move of an opposing attacker, white 4, into a blind-side position against black 10.

The nearest defender's attention is being drawn too much towards the immediate area of action.

He is 'ball watching' when he should be opponent watching.

From his blindside position, black 4 could make an undetected run into very dangerous shooting positions.

It is the goalkeeper's job to sound the alarm and it is the defender's job to listen for it and take notice.

Defending is a matter of collective action and collective responsibility.

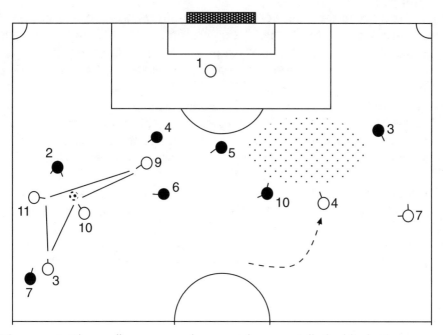

Diagram 4. *The goalkeeper as a player watcher especially for blind side moves.*

In diagram 5, where his team is attacking, the black goalkeeper can see that the backs have lost their concentration and their marking has become slack.

Play may seem so far away that there is no immediate danger.

If the ball is played out to any of the opposing attackers, black 7, 9 and 11, there is little chance of defenders offering an immediate challenge.

Worse, they are unlikely to prevent the attackers from receiving the ball, turning and playing well judged forward passes or dribbling past the defenders.

Teams with great tactical awareness allow opponents to press them back towards their own goal to create just such counter attacking opportunities.

In the same situation, the goalkeeper will demand tight marking against two of the three attackers. One defender, black 2 has held back to provide balance and cover if needed.

Last line balance in defense is usually the responsibility of the defender furthest away from the action: the 'far side' defender as he is known. Responsibility for ultimate cover and balance should, in my view, be shared with the goalkeeper.

Goalkeepers must be educated to assume this responsibility; it will pay huge dividends.

4.2 Limiting Space.

If a goalkeeper can trap and control the ball safely and if he can kick passes with reasonable certainty, there is no reason why he should be confined to his penalty area. Since the change in the laws affecting back pass options, it has become imperative that the goalkeeper's basic footballing skills are absolutely secure and his judgment when and how to use them even more so. Practice has to be adjusted accordingly as we shall see later.

Where a goalkeeper's team has pressed forward to attack the opposing penalty area, quick counter attack by their opponents may require the precise delivery of passes of forty yards or more to achieve penetration behind the backs at speed. Where the target area is beyond the half way line, the distance might be nearer to 50 yards. Fifty yard passes are in the air for a relatively long time, time enough for a goalkeeper with decent out-field techniques to intercept them.

By positioning himself well up-field the goalkeeper will act as a deterrent against long passing counter attacks. No sensible player should hit long, down-field passes straight to an opponent, even to a goalkeeper. . . at least in my team they wouldn't.

If attacking moves become more deliberate and less penetrative, the goalkeeper should gradually retreat towards his normal controlling position in or near to the goal area at a speed to suit the speed of the attack

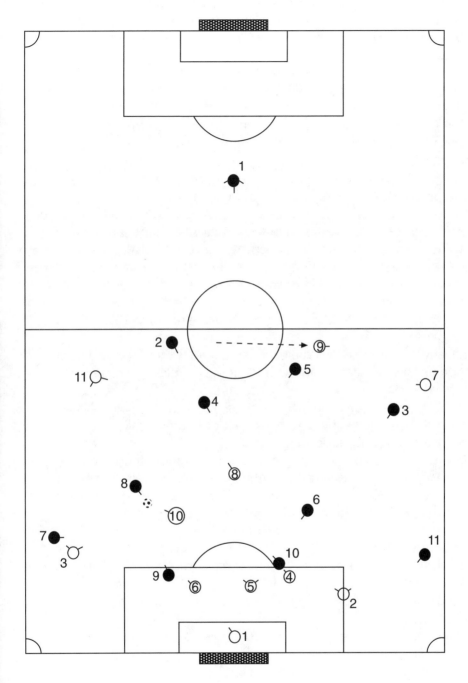

Diagram 5. *The Goalkeeper watching for relaxed (slack) back defenders.*

developing against him. Against skillful players he must always be aware of the possibility of them trying to lob or chip the ball over him, even from considerable distances.

The counter attacking team will play shorter passes. Consequently, defenders should be able to set up pressure points to contain the counter-attack and to re-group.

Some professional coaches used to argue that deploying a goalkeeper in this way was not worth the risk; now they have no choice. The risk is only in the competence of the goalkeeper to intercept the ball and to hit passes safely away from opponents. If coaches can't teach goalkeepers those simple skills they can't teach anyone anything!

Basic to such teaching must be preparing out-field players to offer themselves as targets for passes in sensible positions and, not least, the use of positive communication between the players involved. Where a team plays with a sweeper, the goalkeeper will usually cover against the cross-field pass or switch play. This enables the sweeper to position himself nearer the more direct line of attack and to risk going for interceptions. Here the goalkeeper is in fact taking on the temporary role of 'far side' defender.

Effective security behind the backs encourages them to support counter attacking moves instantly and confidently whenever opportunities occur.

When the goalkeeper makes an interception and gains possession of the ball, his action options should be simplified. His team mates should know what those options are: where he will kick the ball : which players he will look for as targets for kicks or throws.

Passes should rarely if ever be across field unless they are into space behind opposing backs. When intercepted, crossfield passes leave so many players badly positioned to defend. When delivered by a player who is less than expert at hiding his intentions, interception is certain.

4.3 Containment.

The best laid plans can go astray of course and cover may break down.

A goalkeeper may find himself facing an attack which, having caught his backs 'square', has delivered a through pass to a striker moving at speed towards goal.

Does the goalkeeper move out to challenge the attacker or does he delay his challenge in the hope that defenders may recover? What should he do? When and where should he do it?

Hard and fast rules cannot be imposed.

If the goalkeeper feels that the opponent will shoot and that he has an odds on chance of spreading himself at the opponent's feet as he shoots or preferably a split second before, he moves to block the shot. If the attacker is attacking along a line wide of the goal and the goalkeeper has a decent chance of sliding across the opponent and deflecting the ball out of play, so much the better.

If the goalkeeper feels that he can get close enough to the attacker to spread himself at the opponent's feet as or fractionally before his opponent can control or play the ball surely, he goes.

If the attacker is odds on favorite to get possession of the ball and if there is little likelihood of another defender recovering quickly enough to offer any sort of second challenge, the goalkeeper stays. Now he has a different problem; he must try to judge where from and when the attacker will shoot.

It will pay him to make the attacker change his mind.

The goalkeeper needs time: time in which to be as near to the opponent as possible when he shoots: time to get himself into the best possible position to save the shot and time for recovering defenders to give him some kind of cover.

To get more time, the goalkeeper will try to 'con' the attacker into delaying his shot. He might do this by moving out fast only to stop suddenly and back off. Alternatively he might move out cautiously and suddenly back off quickly. He will try to confuse his opponent by changing the 'picture' in front of his opponent unexpectedly. Inevitably some of these moves involve risks and a good goalkeeper never puts all his eggs in the same basket. He must always be prepared to change any tactical move into a dive or jump to save a shot. The attacker, under pressure to score, but faced with a goalkeeper unwilling to 'sell' himself, may take more time over his shot than he can afford. Taking more time may mean that the attacker will find himself much nearer to the goalkeeper than he intended to be and thereby at a serious disadvantage. The nearer to the goalkeeper he is the smaller the goal behind the goalkeeper will seem to be.

4.4 Making an Opponent Change Feet.

Most attackers in 'pressure' situations. . . situations in which they feel expected to score for example. . . will try to use their 'natural' foot.

Moving out towards an attacker running through on goal, the goalkeeper may follow an angle which encourages the attacker to believe that he is being given a chance to shoot with his better foot. At the moment when the goalkeeper thinks that the attacker may be collecting himself for the shot, he moves one step sideways to reduce (narrow) the attacker's shooting angle. What does the attacker do? Continue his shot with his better foot but on a poorer angle or switch the ball to his weaker foot on a better angle? Not an easy decision to make with little or no time to make it.

4.41 Body Language.

Goalkeepers must become students of opponents' body 'speak': their movement mannerisms. All soccer players move, prepare and execute their various skills in unique ways. They have movement 'fingerprints' by which they and their intentions usually can be recognized. All players, but especially goalkeepers, must become students of movement behavior. They need to know what opponents look like when they prepare to shoot: which foot they prefer to use: what is the range of shooting techniques which they have and so on. In all our activities we each develop small, often barely noticeable movement mannerisms or habits which indicate what we are about to do and when we are about to do it. They may be whole body movements, twitches of the leg or foot, movements of the head only or even the most minute movements of the eyes. In soccer, how we begin to swing our foot will show where and how we intend to pass the ball or shoot.

Skillful goalkeepers learn to 'read' these signs and thereby anticipate opponents' actions. But they must be wary, very skillful outfield players learn to use false mannerisms to confuse and mislead opponents.

The game of Soccer may be simple but good players aren't!

4.5 Diving and Jumping To Save.

Inside the penalty area, a goalkeeper's tactical skills are governed by his skill at diving and jumping to catch, punch or deflect the ball safely.

When stretching their arms upwards, most players' elbows are level with the tops of their heads. Assuming that goalkeepers can jump at least as high as other players, they have the advantage of the length of their forearms when moving to catch or punch the ball, if they jump at the right time. In fact most goalkeepers, by training and experience, are better jumpers than most outfield players so the 'keeper's advantages should be substantial.

Nevertheless we often see goalkeepers apparently beaten in the air; outjumped to all intents and purposes.

Goalkeepers will only be beaten in the air when:
1. They have failed to jump at the right time.
2. They have taken off from a standing position rather than from a run.
3. They try to catch the ball at finger tip stretch rather than at palm stretch
4. They fail to jump to meet the ball, to 'attack' it positively, even aggressively.
5. They try to watch the ball and challenging players at the same time.
6. They are fouled.

A goalkeeper cannot control the movements of opponents but goal-keeping tactics must ensure that at least his own players don't obstruct him.

The goalkeeper must be given every opportunity to use his enormous advantages inside the penalty area.

Opponents will stand in his way; they will move down the same line to attack the ball or to hinder him; they will try to disturb the timing of his run and jump by 'faking' similar movements themselves.

They cannot legally hinder, interfere with or in any way physically hamper the goalkeeper when he is attempting to catch or play the ball but they will and more often than not they will get away with it.

Actually blocking a 'keeper's run or getting in the way of his catch unless that opponent is making a genuine effort to play the ball himself, consti-tutes obstruction and is illegal. Unfortunately it happens.

It is difficult for referees to judge the real intentions of players compet-ing for the ball. Attackers may jump for the ball at least as much to put the goalkeeper off as to get to it. For the goalkeeper it's a 'no win' situa-tion but he has to cope with it. To do so he must be absolutely decisive when he chooses from his action options.

4.6 Free Kicks.
4.61 Corner Kicks.
It is bad tactical policy to try to mark opponents who themselves are intent upon inconveniencing the goalkeeper if not actually trying to obstruct him.

Where, for example, two attackers are well inside the goal area and are unmarked, any kick which they can reach in this 'keeper versus two situa-tion, given decent refereeing, should be the goalkeeper's. However, if both opponents are marked the goalkeeper faces a one versus four situa-tion and, decent refereeing or not, is in trouble.

Defensive tactics at a corner kick should enable defenders to cover all spaces into which the ball can be delivered irrespective of where attackers choose to stand.

Opponents are secondary considerations unless they have special per-sonal attributes: extra height, exceptional jumping ability, unusual bravery in getting to unlikely deliveries and so on.

All defenders, the goalkeeper included, should position themselves so that they can attack any crosses from running jumps.

Defenders. . . and goalkeepers. . . who stand within the target areas in the hope that they will win high balls with standing jumps usually don't!

If the goal area is reasonably clear of players and if opposing attackers move into that area to illegally obstruct the goalkeeper, they should be seen easily by the referee, certainly more easily than if several other players are there as well.

Referees must be particularly alert to opponents who stand 'touch tight' in front of goalkeepers. They may seem to move for the same cross but their real intention is to delay their run thereby restricting the run, take off and jump of the goalkeeper; that is obstruction.

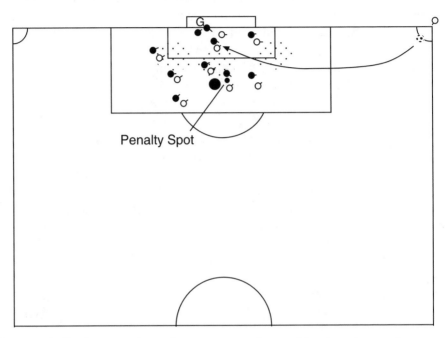

Diagram 6. *Goal area and penalty area congestion and key target areas for an inswinging corner kick, black team defending.*

In diagram 6, three defenders mark three attackers inside the goal area. The accepted key target areas are those shaded; quality goalkeepers are expected to command most of them.

The situation in the goal area near to the goalkeeper is now highly congested. Any movement made by him to command the shaded areas, must take into account intentional or unintentional obstruction by a number of players including his own.

Organizing a defense to cover key areas and important attackers in 'open' play is one thing, covering key areas and important opponents at corner kicks or any other free kicks for that matter is quite another.

The 'keeper must start from a position which will give him the best access to all of the probable target areas. Some, of course, will be more accessible than others and some will be more dangerous than others. A goalkeeper makes his judgment on the basis of probability, the probability that attackers will try to strike from certain areas.

For example, a corner kick taken from the right hand corner with a player's left foot is likely to swing in towards goal. If there is no swing, the probability is that the kick will drop some distance outside the goal area, beyond the goalkeeper's area of responsibility in fact.

The angle of the kicker's approach to the ball together with the power of his kick, estimated from the length of his approach stride and the 'set' of his body, will indicate the probability.

Similarly a kick taken from the same corner but with the kicker's right foot is likely to swing away from the goalkeeper in flight. If it doesn't, the probability is that the kick will travel quite close to the goal again depending on the kicker's angle of approach to the ball and the power with which he kicks it. These are not certainties but they are probabilities.

Nothing can be certain in soccer, it can only be likely.

Organizing a defense to cover key areas against a corner kick is one thing, covering key areas and important opponents during free play is quite another.

In free play, of course, the player with the ball can change the whole situation by moving the ball a few inches this way or that. Indeed by transferring the ball from foot to foot he will change the probable flight path and the dropping zone of the ball any number of times. Reading his intentions will not be easy, nevertheless the position from which a cross is likely and the player's approach to the ball will indicate certain probabilities for the goalkeeper's benefit.

Like all good players, the 'keeper will build up his own mental filing system of different players' capabilities: their body languages. His expanding experience will help him to calculate the probable results of various action options.

Look and learn (and remember!) certainly applies to goalkeeping.

Corners taken with the 'other foot' i.e. right foot from the left corner will, in all likelihood, be inswingers with the target areas close to or actually inside the goal area and of course vice versa.

Attacking tactics may be to move three attackers into the goal area and hope that they will be followed by three opponents as in diagram 6. If a defender covers each post, that means that there will be at least four defenders, including the goalkeeper, inside that area. The attackers will be looking for flick headers, rebounds, deflections; anything directed towards goal. Personally I would deploy a surprise jumper, someone not particularly tall or known for his jump heading ability but capable of making a decent jump from a ten yard approach run.

In the congestion to which the goal area is being subjected a surprise jumper might offer the greatest reward.

In any event, the greater the number of players inside the goal area the greater the problems for the goalkeeper.

Even though intimidated by a crowd of players, almost half of them his own, it is still the responsibility of the goalkeeper to sort out the problem and to spot the likelihood of an attacker coming in late.

In fact the goalkeeper might be significantly helped if most, even all his defenders left the goal area to him. Fewer players would mean fewer obstacles and with only attackers in the goal area even referees with less than perfect vision might be better able to see whatever sharp practice was going on.

Orthodox corner kicks might produce player deployments as in diagram 7.

The target areas achievable with very little change (Diagrams 8 and 9) in the kicking action are much larger than those for inswinging corner kicks. While the goalkeeper is less likely to be called upon to deal with outswinging corners, there is always the possibility of the target being the 'near post' and also the switch from a swerved kick to a straight drive can be achieved relatively easily with only a slight modification of kicking action. The goalkeeper is the defensive controller in these circumstances and must communicate with his co-defenders accordingly, calmly and confidently. . . even if he isn't!

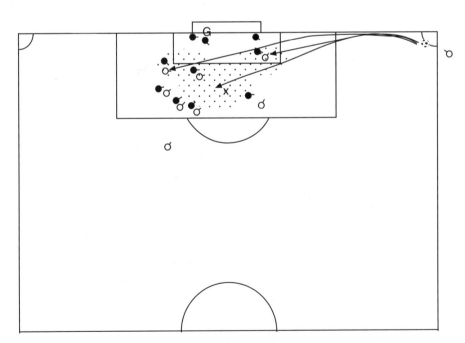

Diagram 7. *Orthodox player deployment for an outswinging corner kick (goalkeeper: 'G').*

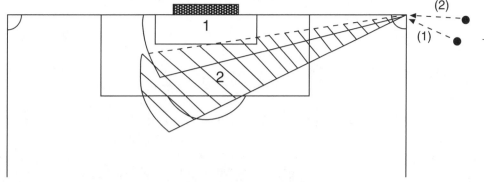

Diagram 8. *Corner kicks. Alteration to the kicker's approach angle and its effect on target sector: outswinging kicks.*

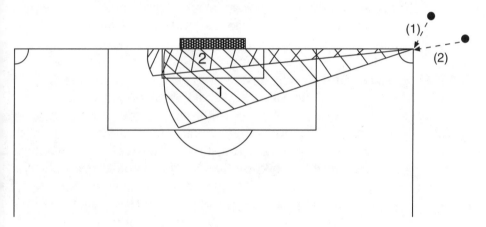

Diagram 9. *Corner Kicks. The effect of approach angles on target sectors: inswinging kicks.*

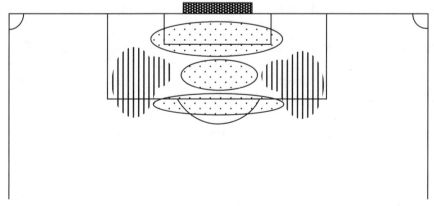

Diagram 10. *Heavily defended areas (dotted). Thinly defended areas (lined).*

The time available to the goalkeeper is not merely the product of the distance the ball must travel and the power behind the kick. The kicker must take time to assess the target areas and players, also he must take time to actually prepare himself to kick the ball. These acts demand concentration. In any case, the kicker must attend to what he is doing, not to what the goalkeeper, perhaps 45 yards away, may be doing.

This is the time when, having decided upon the various probabilities and so late as to be unseen by the kicker, the goalkeeper may begin to make his move. That move may mean a five yard start in the race for the ball.

Five yards start in any race, usually, should be a winning start.

Goalkeepers, expert at using these tactics, are those who appear from nowhere, apparently, to catch the ball ten yards or more from their goal lines.

Anticipation, based upon clever interpretation of the probabilities open to opponents, is perhaps the single most important tactical skill available to a goalkeeper.

4.611 Adverse Ground Conditions.

These may be 'heavy', i.e. have a sticky, holding attachment to boots, and make running difficult and hard work. Alternatively the ground may be wet and slippery making ball movement significantly quicker and to that extent less readable. Firm but frozen top surfaces make player movement tentative and uncertain while bumpy, hard surfaces make ball behavior unpredictable. All of these affect a goalkeeper's capabilities and many defenders (and coaches) look to goalkeepers with unreasonable expectations for defensive security. Goalkeepers' problems are just as great as any other player's, his footwork just as apprehensive and his jumping ability significantly handicapped in some cases.

If three or four defenders are positioned on the goal line and inside the goal they are likely to be accompanied by a similar number of attackers: more trouble.

It may pay a goalkeeper to position himself with a significant start advantage for attacking likely dropping zones. Defenders who will drop back onto the goal line will position themselves some way off it initially, only dropping back when the kick has been struck.

They may get away with it, they may not. Certainly such advantages as the goalkeeper may be perceived as having will become more realistic when he has been given total license to say what he wants from his co-defenders.

Broadly speaking, on adverse ground conditions, a ball struck hard towards goal will pose greater problems for defenders who have less time to meet any threat and also have unreliable footholds. The goalkeeper can do no better than get his angles right and move to reduce the distance between himself and an opponent playing the ball towards goal or shooting. At that time he needs defenders covering behind him. He must be the first shot or deflection stopper.

4.612 Wind.
Strong wind blowing towards goal, especially if it is gusty, requires a goalkeeper to delay any movement to attack the ball. When he moves for the ball he will need covering players nearby rather than on the goal line. Defenders nearby should try to protect him from interference by opponents. These are circumstances when an opponent 'making a back' by moving underneath a jumping goalkeeper is guilty of seriously dangerous foul play but these players are about.

Most goalkeepers I know prefer a wind blowing the ball in towards goal than away from it and thereby towards oncoming attackers. A wind taking the ball away from a goalkeeper trying to jump to catch or punch, presents a much more difficult judgment problem than vice versa.

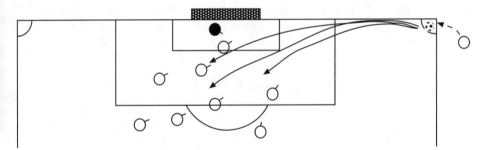

Diagram 11. *Alignment of attackers for wind assisted outswinging corner kicks.*

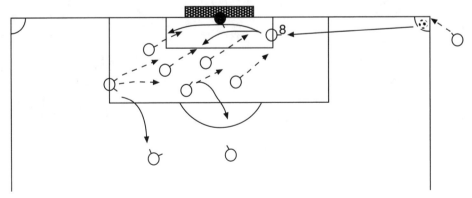

Diagram 12. *Attacking deployment for a wind assisted corner kick attackers give themselves longer runs into take off to jump areas.*

Defense will be more secure where supporting defenders remain grounded looking for shot blocking positions rather than trying to jump to assist the goalkeeper. Centre backs of some size jumping to attack a cross with the goalkeeper are more likely to hinder than help him. After all, if a goalkeeper with a two foot stretch height advantage over all other players can't win the ball, what makes a player able to use only his head think that he can?

Throws In.

Throws aimed for the goal area should present no problems: they shouldn't but they do. The ball is in the air much longer than for a corner kick and that extra time should be goalkeeper 'travel time'. He should command back header threats from any attacker inside the goal area. It is the responsibility of referees to see any attempt to interfere with his movement to attack the ball. Target attackers moving to receive the throw and flick the ball behind them should be marked only if they move to the extreme forward edge of the goal area. Diagram 13.

Too many defenses, including goalkeepers, are organized to deal with the results of back headers rather than their source. Goalkeepers worth the name and starting from near post positions should 'eat' long throws. In fact it is an insult to require them to do anything other than that.

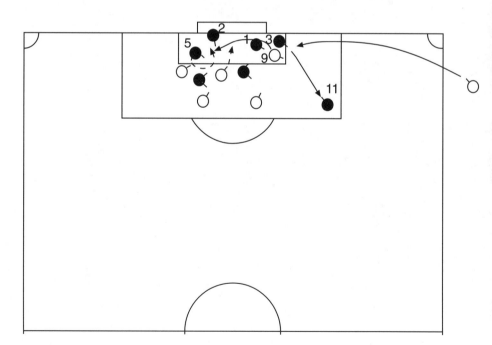

Diagram 13. *Goalkeeper and backdefenders positioned to deal with long throw in dangers, specifically flick on headers, white O.*

4.62 Direct Free-kicks Close to Goal.

The improvement in the ratio of goals scored to the number of set plays taken near to the penalty area, including corners and free kicks, has been considerable during the past twenty years.

As success brought huge financial rewards, general defensive play received concentrated scrutiny from professional coaches world wide.

As the game took on a high profile through world exposure on television, scoring goals. . . indeed creating shooting opportunities. . . became increasingly rare.

One of few responses, in professional soccer, has been to become more efficient in using set-play situations where the attacking side can control and time the action to suit itself to a great extent.

There is still room for improvement.

Many coaches in England, 'backed' by the revelations of statisticians, at best speculative and at worst spurious, extended their robotic control over players at set plays to similar control in free play.

Hence the development in England of predictable play and, much more serious, unimaginative, highly predictable players.

The best strategy for dealing with free kicks near to the penalty area is not to give them away.

Skillful defense is based upon disciplined individual and team organization. The height of irresponsibility must be to lose discipline and give away free kicks in dangerous areas. Attacking tactics for any free-kick near to the penalty area will aim to produce a shot at goal first or second touch or, very rarely. . . and then only by highly skillful players. . . from a third touch.

Broadly speaking, the greater the number of touches and players involved in playing the ball, the greater the probability of the shot missing goal or being blocked.

4.621 Tactical Problems.

The goalkeeper's tactical problems will be affected by:
   a) The angle at which the kick is being taken, if a direct shot is attempted.
   b) The angle from which the shot is likely to be taken if second or third touches are involved.
   c) The distance between the ball and the goalkeeper.
   d) The view which the goalkeeper has of the ball and of the players who are likely to be involved in moves related to the kick.
   e) Ground and weather conditions which are likely to limit or extend the attackers' tactical options.
   f) The extent to which the referee is tolerant or strict in the matter of

taking the kick.

e.g. Does he demand that opponents are exactly ten yards (9.15m.) from the ball?

Does he permit opponents to attack the ball before the actual kicking contact is made?

To what extent does he permit attackers to try to restrict the goalkeeper's view of the action or to disturb the defensive wall?

Any respectable goalkeeper should save a high proportion of direct shots from thirty yards or more, in any 'shoot-out' between himself and a single striker.

In fact I would wager that out of twenty such shots he wouldn't have to save a good many: the striker would miss the goal.

4.622 Defensive Walls; Pros and Cons.

With a wall of players in front of him, the goalkeeper might save fewer rather than more!

For any number of reasons, the wall can be a serious handicap to a goalkeeper, the player it is most designed to help.

The wall may unsight the 'keeper. It may cause him to take up a position from which certain areas of the goal become relatively less accessible.

And rather than discourage the player taking the kick, a wall may give the striker useful markers for judging his target more effectively!

Add to these the possibility of players 'ducking out' when needed to block a fierce shot and the value of a human wall diminishes.

A free shot on the other hand might frighten the striker into excessive caution. He might think. . . and he could be right. . . that his team mates and all the fans expect him to score easily.

Great expectations create pressure and nervous insecurity.

Penalty kicks. . . free shots at goal from only twelve yards. . . raise the expectations of everyone except the kicker. He knows that it's not as easy as it looks!

Expectations exert powerful influences on all sports stars.

Understanding their causes and effects is one of the keys to successful coaching at all levels of the game.

At a direct free kick, up to thirty metres from goal, an apparently impregnable human wall may inspire the kicker to 'go for it' and shoot with 'bend' and 'dip' for the remotest corners of the goal.

The greater the challenge to a player' skills, the more successful he may become in overcoming that challenge. And it's up to his coach to challenge him. . . or his mother!

Defensive 'walls' have come to be regarded as providing ultimate security at free-kick situations; they don't and can't!

Ultimate security is in the hands. . . literally. . . of the goalkeeper.

A wall, if used, must be regarded only as a help to the goalkeeper. If it isn't a help but a hindrance it should be reconstructed or done away with.

Too often the wall is used as an excuse by goalkeepers for failing to do their jobs. . . to stop scoring shots!

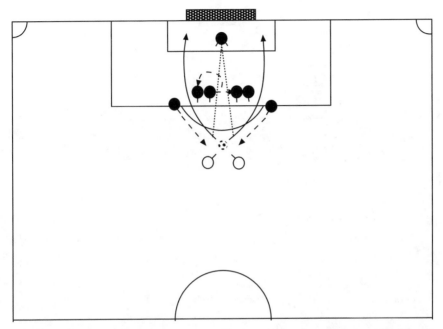

Diagram 14. *A direct free kick at 25 yards faced by a four player wall with a central observation 'hole'.*

In diagram 14, a direct free kick has been awarded about 25 yards from goal and central to it.

Faced with a shot at this range in open play, the goalkeeper might be perhaps three to six yards off his line in a central position.

For this free kick, he might prefer to be two or three yards off his line; any more and he might be 'chipped'. . . beaten by a shot over his head.

4.623 The Split Wall.

A four or five player defensive wall should block any kick aimed straight and direct at goal from 25 yards. It should also block powerfully swerved kicks aimed at the extreme limits of the goal. An observation hole can be created late and the wall reinforced to one side or the other as a player moves out of the hole position and onto the end of the wall.

To be positioned to save in any direction and therefore to see what is going on, the 'keeper' needs this one player gap in the centre of the wall at the moment when the kicker moves into his last couple of strides.

If the gap is made too soon, opponents are likely to fill it themselves, which in itself is the best possible argument for having one!

A split wall accommodates the goalkeeper's best position to cope with direct, straight or swerved shots at goal.

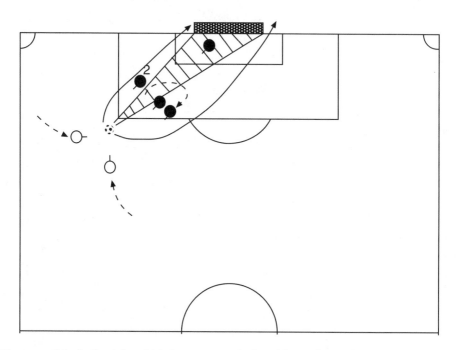

Diagram 15. *A direct free kick from an angle faced by a three player wall with a 'hole'. The shaded area is the minimum to be countered by the wall. The wall is built on black 2's position.*

In diagram 15, the kick is to be taken at an angle to the goal: the angle reduces the need for a full size wall. The kick taker may switch the kick to a team mate with a better shooting angle and to surprise the defenders. The goalkeeper needs to be given every opportunity to see this switch and the 'new' kicker's feet. Feint moves amount to nothing when the kicker has to kick the ball. The longer the goalkeeper's view of a player's preparation for actual contact with the ball, the better his chance of 'reading' the shot accurately.

4.624 Constructing a Wall.

Generally speaking, in high class soccer the wall is built on the position taken up by one defender whose body 'width' is outside the goal post nearer to the ball, black 2 in diagram 15.

The remaining players build the wall inside this 'key' player to block ball flight to as much of the goal as the goalkeeper wants covered.

In fact, the goalkeeper should position himself to save shots as if the wall was not there. The wall is then constructed on what might be called secondary, security requirements.

Too often walls are constructed in the hope of providing total security.

Smart goalkeepers go along with the idea because it gives them excuses for letting in free kicks.

Human walls set-up at free-kicks can never give perfect cover: nor can goalkeepers. Shots hit with pace and swerve into the extreme top corners of the goal will score and deserve to.

4.63 Medium Range Direct Free Kicks.
Penalty area tactics for any free kick likely to be aimed there from medium to long range (40 yards +) should be designed to enable the goalkeeper to get to the ball first if at all possible.

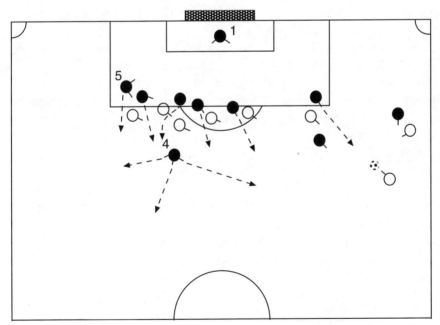

Diagram 16. *Moving out to trap opponents offside. The duties and responsibilities or 'fair-safe' defenders.*

4.631 'Fail-safe' Controllers.
In diagram 16, the defense has lined up tightly against their opponents. When the kicker is committed to the kick, i.e. when he is two strides from planting his non-kicking foot, and on a signal, they will move forward very

quickly. Black 5 is the controlling player here; he alone will recover against anything unexpected.

An auxiliary security player, black 4 marks no one and is positioned where he can see and track any opponent likely to make a run towards the target area from a deep position. The player assuming this role needs to be absolutely sure in the use of his 'inside' foot, the foot nearer to his goal-keeper. The angle of the free kick on his goal and his position in relation to the angle of delivery determines that. His 'inside' foot is the one most easily used and most likely to be needed should he have to play the ball urgently.

4.64 Indirect Free Kicks Inside The Penalty Area.

All players must be at least ten yards from the ball when a free kick is taken or, if the kick is nearer to the goal than ten yards, they may stand on the goal line itself.

Where the kick is ten yards or more from the goal, a defensive wall will be formed ELEVEN yards from the ball. The wall must be big enough, i.e. incorporate enough players, to cover the width of the whole goal; probably eight players will be involved.

A direct shot cannot be taken and players not in the wall will be positioned TEN yards from the ball and prepared to challenge the most likely player to whom the ball may be played.

Whatever the size of the wall, the goalkeeper will be positioned on the best possible angle to the kick and TEN yards from the ball, as if he was facing the kick alone.

The goalkeeper has the best chance of saving shots certain to be hit as hard as possible: in first class soccer that's very hard indeed!

Wall players must be brave enough to block shots with ALL body parts some, unfortunately, badly designed for that purpose and excluding the hands or arms.

Facing close-range, indirect, free kicks, keepers are allowed to dive in any direction including forwards to block a shot. Some referees allow goalkeepers to move forward to block shots slightly before kicks are taken; they shouldn't but they do. Goalkeepers can't expect such generosity but they will be grateful should it happen.

4.65 Penalty Kicks.

Goalkeepers now may move before the kickers contact the ball when taking penalties. In more than forty years experience of topsoccer, six of those as a professional player, I never saw a penalty kick taken correctly within the laws of the game!

Without exception, goalkeepers have been allowed to move their feet

. . . even considerable distances. . . before kickers have made contact with the ball: more often than not a long time before.

This was illegal but goalkeepers now must take whatever advantage they can.

Basically there are two kinds of penalty takers. The first has decided and practiced what he will do. He always does the same thing which, probably, is to drive the ball as hard as he can to hit the inside of the side netting.

Observant goalkeepers know that he takes the kick with the same foot and aims usually for one side of the goal but occasionally the other.

This player knows that a shot hit low and hard at a known target will beat any goalkeeper even IF that goalkeeper is allowed to move before the ball is kicked.

The goalkeeper who knows where and how the kicker operates may move to a position on the goal line one or two yards towards the assumed direction of the kick to tempt the kicker to change his mind and target.

Making a 'spot' kicker change his mind is more than half-way to winning the battle of minds in which the goalkeeper starts off with an enormous psychological advantage; no-one expects HIM to be successful!

The second type of kicker is the 'placer' who depends upon a number of kicking options. . . perhaps two or three. . . placed with the greatest possible accuracy, just inside the goal posts, but at the expense of great power.

The 'placer' is as much concerned with reading the goalkeeper's intentions as the 'keeper is with reading his.

The time to disturb this player's concentration is as he begins to lower his head to concentrate on a perfect contact with the ball.

With his head down and his concentration in sharp focus, he is unlikely to see any move by the goalkeeper, unless his attention is drawn deliberately.

During the kicker's run up, the goalkeeper may shift his weight, possibly raising his arm slightly in the same direction, to give the impression of an early directional commitment to save. The shift of weight must keep the goalkeeper's centre of gravity within the base made by his feet all the time. If his centre of gravity moves outside or towards the edge of his base too quickly, the goalkeeper may not be able to correct his balance in time to take off in the required direction.

Additionally, the goalkeeper should be moving up and down on the balls of his feet slightly as transfer of weight takes place. He needs to overcome the inertia produced by the gravitational 'pull' of his body weight when stationary, while moving sideways stealthily almost imperceptibly.

Some goalkeepers gamble by making extravagant 'fake' movements early, in the hope that they will cause the kicker to change his target and that they will be able to re-establish an effective take-off base in time.

Whatever the tactics chosen, it will pay handsome dividends for a goal-keeper to practice and perfect his tactical options.

As I have said, the most successful of all tactics involving all free kicks, but penalties more than most, is not to give them away!

Nevertheless, expert penalty and free-kick saving goalkeepers are worth their weights in gold.

4.7 Shot Stopping.

There is a great deal more to goalkeeping than stopping shots, neverthe-less goalkeepers worth the name must be very good at it.

Successful shot stopping involves the following factors:

4.71 'Reading' Probabilities.

Good goalkeepers calculate a shot's direction from watching how the attacker's foot seems likely to make contact with the ball.

Whatever else has to be taken into account, it is the actual contact between foot (or head) and ball and the line along which the attacker applies the force of his strike which determines where the shot will go.

Reading the shooting line and angle means waiting until the last split second before impact before making a final judgment. Skillful strikers can and do change their foot-to-ball contact during that time thereby kicking the ball in an entirely different direction and they have to be outstandingly skillful to do it.

4.72 Reacting and Anticipating.

'Reacting' means waiting for the split second of actual contact, when the striker is fully committed, and when the 'keeper' is sure that he knows where the shot will go.

'Anticipating' means reading all the clues which the striker reveals, estimating the probabilities and making an intelligent guess at the striker's target.

Some goalkeepers are gamblers; they can't be bothered to watch and wait. Gambling goalkeepers make spectacular saves from time to time but they never develop the air of massive certainty which is the mark of an exceptional goalkeeper.

Lev Yashin, a Russian goalkeeping colossus during the early sixties and among the best three goalkeepers that I ever saw, was a past master at 'out- waiting' opponents. He waited, tall and broad, in front of attackers, appearing to grow to a monstrous size, until THEY were compelled to make the first move. . . usually too late.

Yashin's patience, together with a genius for calculating shooting 'angles', was matchless.

Some goalkeepers have gambling instincts, great goalkeepers never. They only take a risk when there is no other option and then only after carefully and quickly calculating the odds.

4.73 Ball Watching.

Outfield players who are 'ball watchers' are dangerous players. . . to their own team. Hypnotized by the ball, they fail to understand that the ball is never dangerous. It's the players who are waiting for it who set the real problems.

Goalkeepers, however, must be good ball and player watchers. The ball, and saving shots or getting possession of it, is what their job is all about.

Being in position to see the ball, wherever it is, whoever has it, is vital to sound goalkeeping. Goalkeepers must be able to see around corners . . . literally. A goalkeeper must be able to bend or stretch, without reducing his ability to run, jump, or dive to save, to track the ball behind other players. He must do it without losing the position of balance on the balls of his feet which enables him to explode into action in a fraction of a second.

4.74 'Standing Up' To Save.

Staying on his feet until the attacker makes his strike at the ball, waiting until the last possible moment before deciding what action to take, is the 'Yashin factor' referred to earlier. Strikers produce all kinds of fake moves or dummies to get the goalkeeper off balance and moving in the wrong direction. Any directional move by the goalkeeper is the wrong move for the goalkeeper and the right one for the attacker.

It is important for goalkeepers to develop the patience to refuse the temptation to move first.

It is equally important that goalkeepers master the skills of throwing dummies themselves. Attacker and goalkeeper, each is trying to out guess the other to compel him to make the first move. Goalkeepers who are too quick to dive or to drop are 'easy meat' for patient strikers.

4.75 Multiple Saves.

Having made one save, a goalkeeper must prepare immediately to make another. . . or others! On many occasions a goalkeeper may make a superb stop but cannot hold the ball. He must react like lightning to secure possession before a goal area prowler can get his foot to the ball. The best way of learning how to stop shots is to practice the art of shooting! One of the best goalkeepers I had the pleasure of playing with as a schoolboy and as a professional, played junior representative soccer as both goalkeeper and as a centre forward. . . but not at the same time!

When you think about it, the best way of gaining a deep insight into the positional problems and possibilities of any position on a soccer field is by seeking experience in that position.

As a wise, old Indian friend of mine said, "To become a good fisherman you must think like a fish".

Central defenders should practice occasionally as central strikers and vice versa: similarly with goalkeepers.

Outstanding goalkeepers have fast feet and fast hands, much like great boxers in fact.

Making 'reaction' saves in quick succession is only possible when a goalkeeper's feet are on the ground ready for the next move.

He must be on the move but the movements of his feet must enable him always to be in contact with the ground, on the balls of his feet and ready to push off with maximum thrust in any required direction.

Chapter 5
Goalkeeping
Techniques and Skills

Techniques in soccer are those actions involving the player and the ball with or without the presence of opposing players. Skill is the use or application of technique in a situation in which team mates or opponents or both are present.

In other words, skill involves techniques applied in realistic situations. The difference is important for coaches who accept responsibility for increasing the range of techniques and the quality of skills available to their individual players.

In modern soccer too much practice attention is paid to team tactical cleverness which fails often because of the technical deficiencies of players.

There is all the difference in the world between pure technical practice and practice devised to transfer technical competence into true skill.

The first you can do on your own or with or without a coach. All that you need is a wall, the will to practice and the imagination to 'see' yourself using your practice skills, totally successfully, in the game.

The world of fantasy is a world in which all aspiring sports stars must spend a great deal of their young lives.

The second kind of practice, skill practice, involves players applying techniques while learning to 'read' and control complex situations. Effective skill practice, which means real learning, has to be carefully set up, intelligently directed and easily repeated as often as may be necessary. Co-operating and opposing players are required to make realistic but controlled contributions.

This kind of practice is known as functional practice.

This is what only a real coach can do. Coaches whose imaginations never extend beyond hard physical training, so called skill drills and six a side play are kidding themselves and their players.

There is a lot of them about.

Learning and therefore effective practice rarely occurs by chance.

5.1 Catching and Fielding.

Catching is receiving and holding the ball in the hands.

Fielding involves receiving and channeling the ball via the hands and arms into the lower body.

A goalkeeper must catch and hold the ball securely while standing, kneeling, falling, diving, rolling, running and jumping and often while doing two or three of those actions at the same time.

Safe fielding and secure ball holding is demanded when shots are driven hard along what may be a bumpy, dry (or frozen) surface: a bumpy and heavy surface: a muddy surface: a flat, well-grassed surface: a flat and greasy, wet surface; in fact any combination of 'natural' ground conditions from water-saturated to desert-dry.

There are certain principles governing sound techniques, irrespective of individual goalkeeping styles or idiosyncrasies.

First, a goalkeeper must ensure that as much of his body as possible is between the goal and the ball when he receives it.

He may 'field' the ball using a standing channel.

He may have the time or need to use a kneeling channel.

Whichever technique he uses he MUST set up a secondary barrier, some other part of his body, behind his hands. Both his hands and the secondary barrier must be relaxed enough to absorb the impact of the ball. There must be little if any possibility for the ball to rebound out of control.

The harder the stopping surface, the greater the likelihood of an uncontrollable rebound.

It is important that goalkeepers develop the habit of closing all possible gaps between say the feet, the knees, the arms and the sides of the body. All fielding positions look, and are, solid and impregnable.

The actions, simple or acrobatic, of great goalkeepers never look 'sloppy', or untidy. They make saving shots look easy, often effortless but never 'chancy'.

It is not easy to be absolutely precise about catching techniques. Goalkeepers have hands of various sizes and shapes and use them accordingly. Big hands may be an advantage but hand size alone is no guarantee of security in catching. Catching and holding the ball is more a matter for the fingers than for the palms of the hands. Fingers because we are born with an instinct to grasp anything which touches our hands.

When catching a soccer ball both hands are presented so that they form an open 'basket'. The thumbs are touching when the catch is made with the fingers pointing upwards (a baseball catch).

The little fingers are touching when the catch is made with the fingers pointing downwards. Until the goalkeeper is committed to one or the other, his fingers will be relaxed, pointing towards play (the ball) but outwards.

Keeping fingers out of the way of the ball until they actually close round it is important. 'Ball catchers' in many sports have learned that to their cost. . . painfully!

5.11 Catching, Jumping and Diving.

Catching the ball when jumping or diving, often at full stretch, poses special problems. . . for the goalkeeper's forearms and elbows!

When jumping vertically to catch, the forearms are kept parallel. This enables the hands and fingers to form the basket referred to earlier.

If the elbows are moved further apart the hands tend to turn backwards and behind the ball making the 'grasp reflex' difficult to employ.

If the elbows are forced towards each other, too much, the hands tend to turn inwards and the ball can be held only at the sides. Trying to catch a wet or greasy ball like this often results in it slipping through the catching 'basket'. Diving at full stretch to catch is a different matter.

The danger now is to lose sight of the ball. This can happen when the goalkeeper begins to bring up his arms for the catch while diving.

The 'keeper's top arm moves across his eyes and creates a temporary, blind spot. He loses sight of the ball at a time when he needs to be judging the ball's movement in flight very carefully.

To avoid producing a 'blind spot', the first movement of his top arm must be over his head. His arms now make a 'window' through which he keeps the ball in view while making his dive.

Having caught the ball, when jumping high or diving, the goalkeeper must pull the ball down and into the security of his stomach quickly.

There are occasions when the goalkeeper has to improvise; when he sees the ball late or when he has been caught in two minds.

That's when basics count. First he has to stop the ball. . . with as much 'body' behind it as possible. Second he has to secure possession decisively.

A shot traveling at chest height may be fielded, i.e. channeled into the stomach, by jumping so that the reception area is lined up with the flight path of the ball. Alternatively the goalkeeper may bend his knees and use the 'baseball catch', possibly deflecting the ball onto the ground before catching it first bounce.

There are additional problems to solve when jumping high or diving at full stretch to catch the ball.

Both jumps and dives must employ optimum explosive force (power) at take-off if the ball is to be caught as high (early) as possible.

Irrespective of jumping or diving style, the generation of optimum force at take-off is governed by certain 'laws of human motion'.

First, the goalkeeper must be already moving before he explodes into his jump or dive. If he is still, i.e. inert, he will need that much more power to get airborne and he is likely to be fractionally late.

Remember the reference to 'fast feet' earlier? For both boxers and goalkeepers, fast feet means moving feet! The neuro-motor system has to be activated before it can do its job. Keeping it ticking over is the answer.

Second, if activation includes a run, a skip or even at worst a shuffle before take-off, the jump or dive will cover a significantly increased distance or height.

Watch the feet of top tennis players waiting to receive a serve, even the worst of them might earn good money as tap dancers.

Third, the take-off for a jump is more effective off one foot than off two. A run is more easily transferred into a one foot take-off than into a double footed take-off. The up-swing of the arms and the free leg are important in gaining optimum height.

Fourth, to develop optimum thrust in one direction the neuro-muscular system employs a 'recoil' mechanism. The initial movement 'inclination' is away from the proposed direction of dive. This is why the Olympic sprinter goes back on his blocks fractionally before generating forward thrust. The muscles generating thrust need to 'gather' themselves before acting on the athlete's limbs to initiate movement.

This means that a goalkeeper must be careful when using 'feints'. Some goalkeepers become very clever at 'throwing feints' to make attackers shoot in directions for which the keepers are prepared. 'Feinting' to save means transferring weight in one direction while preparing for a move in some other direction. If an attacker calls the keeper's bluff and shoots in the direction of the feint, the goalkeeper may be totally unbalanced. His weight is likely to be over his 'wrong' foot; wrong that is for push off.

Balanced equally and easily over both feet; using small, side to side swaying movements but above all with his feet on the move, the keeper has the best chance for covering all his options fast.

For similar reasons, arm movements should be minimal until the final commitment to go for the ball is made.

5.12 Landing.

Controlling the landing after a powerful jump or dive to catch the ball is as important as making the catch and perhaps even more difficult.

Falls or dives, often from significant heights, can be painful. Injuries may result unless the technique for absorbing the shock of landing is learned. Even worse, the landing may knock the ball out of the 'keeper's grasp.

When making a high catch, contact with players jumping late and beneath him may cause a goalkeeper to be turned in the air; a controlled landing may be difficult. He must be prepared to tuck up with his landing and roll off whatever part of his body touches down first. Holding the ball in both hands he may, at best, use only his foot or part of his lower leg to break his fall. Some top flight 'keepers can control the ball in one hand while using the other to absorb the shock of hitting the dirt. If the goalkeeper feels himself being turned in the air, he should try to land on one side of his body, rolling and pulling the ball into his stomach at the same time as he touches down.

Attackers who deliberately move beneath a jumping goalkeeper do so to turn him in the air. They know that he will land without any control, often on his head or upper body. Forgive the repetition but 'making a back' as it is called is one of the most serious fouls in soccer. Those practicing it should be dismissed without further warning and banned from the game for a long time.

There is nothing worse in sport than a player taking advantage of an opponent's unprotectable position to deliberately injure him. I have no reservations about calling it what it is, 'g. b. h., grievous bodily harm'.

Goalkeepers, with large hands, manage to use the ball and their forearms as shock absorbers. . . or landing 'wheels'. Their grasp on the ball has to be very secure: the whip-lash effect of landing with outstretched arms may shake the ball out of the strongest grip.

Ball protection comes before a comfortable landing. Goalkeeping isn't for players looking for comfortable and peaceful lives.

When diving to land while holding the ball, a goalkeeper tries to land sideways to the ground; never face and chest downwards.

If he lands forearms first, the shock of landing will be reduced. As the rest of his body hits the dirt, shock vibrations pass down his body, through his legs and away from the ball. If he lands with legs and lower body first, followed by his arms and hands, the shock wave passes up his body, through his hands and towards the ball.

This, as we have already seen, is likely to shake the ball free of the 'keeper's grasp.

5.2 Punching and Palming Clear.

Whenever a goalkeeper can catch the ball he must. When he can't he must deflect or punch the ball towards safety, usually out of play.

If he is likely to be under severe pressure, fair or unfair, he plays safe by punching the ball clear of the penalty area or by palming the ball out of play over the goal-line.

Punching the ball is best achieved using a one handed punch, even when the ball is traveling directly towards him over the heads of the central backs.

If a goalkeeper is able to punch the ball with two fists, almost certainly he is in a position to catch it!

Only when opposing players are intent upon interfering with him, legally or otherwise, is the punch the better option and referees should quickly put a stop to the 'otherwise'.

The take off is one footed and the 'free' leg swing is up and across the body to give optimum protection to the goalkeeper's more sensitive parts.

This protective move is made easier by the body twist which precedes a one handed punch. The free arm, the arm nearer to other jumpers, can be used as a 'fender' against physical contact from defenders and attackers. It is likely to happen! The punch is delivered, with the knuckles, through the ball. For optimum effect, the knuckles should follow through in the direction required and they should remain in contact with the ball for as long as possible.

Having punched clear the goalkeeper must resume his ready to save position instantly. . . or quicker! The clearance may be returned as a shot or as a lob almost immediately and he has to be positioned to deal with it.

When the ball is delivered into the penalty area from the flanks, the goalkeeper is helped because he is already sideways onto his direction of punch.

The disadvantage is the probability that he must punch across the ball's line of flight. This involves risk, especially in wet and greasy conditions. It may pay him to punch the ball in the direction from which it came.

His co-defenders must understand their goalkeeper's problems and his probable personal tactics.

The right kind of goalkeeping gloves can be vital.

They must have catching and punching surfaces which are 'tacky', that is to say non-slip, while the glove as a whole must be soft enough to allow the 'keeper to have maximum 'feel' when catching and holding the ball.

Goalkeeping gloves. . . the good ones that is. . . must enable the wearer to handle the ball in all conditions significantly more securely and effectively: in fact as if he didn't have any gloves on.

Protecting the goalkeeper's hands is a secondary consideration.

In recent times goalkeepers, short of spending money, have endorsed gloves which are more deserving of designer labels than of ball catching and punching credibility. Most would have served Mohammed Ali better than any self respecting 'keeper.

Deflecting the ball or 'palming' it away is a very important technique and requires extremely skillful judgment.

Usually it is used when, having dived at full stretch, a goalkeeper knows that catching the ball and landing with it cannot be guaranteed. With arms fully stretched, he can rarely use them to push the ball away. He has to use the pace of the ball to help him to guide it to safety and out of play.

He will extend the palms and fingers of his saving hand backwards as he makes contact with the ball which will, in effect, slide off his fingers and away from them at an angle.

If he misjudges the ball's pace he is likely to find the ball still in play and closer to goal.

When in doubt an experienced goalkeeper will play safe and rarely allow himself to be drawn into a dive at maximum stretch. He will always dive with his elbows slightly bent to enable him to give extra push to the ball to deflect it out of play, if needed.

Occasionally, where a strong wind is carrying the ball towards goal the goalkeeper will find himself in a 'no win' situation.

Where physical challenge, whatever its form, occurs near to his goal line, a goalkeeper is best advised to palm the ball over the bar and out of play. Positioned facing a high cross, it is probable that his outside arm, the arm furthest from the goal-line, will give him the most controlled and highest swing to guide the ball over the cross-bar.

Hard and fast rules cannot be laid down. The goalkeeper must improvise and adapt to circumstances as they arise. Nevertheless certain basic skills have been tried and tested over the years. Practicing them will pay off.

5.3 Goalkeeping Angles and Diving at Feet.
When a goalkeeper is faced by an opponent moving towards goal and about to shoot, he must act on certain priorities. Respecting these priorities may not prevent a goal from being scored but it will make scoring as difficult as the circumstances allow.

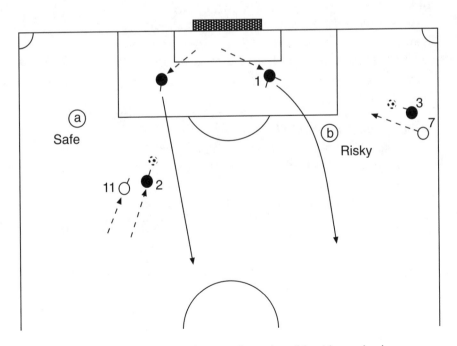

Diagram 17. *(a) narrow angle goalkeeper clearance. (b) wide angle clearance.*

First, the goalkeeper must move towards the attacker on an angle which enables him to block out most or all of the attacker's sight of the goal.

Second, moving closer to the attacker while the attacker is preparing to shoot will significantly improve the goalkeeper's chances of blocking the shot at the attacker's feet or of making him change his mind about shooting at all.

When he is about to shoot, making a striker change his mind is very good goalkeeping.

Third, as he moves to 'angle' the attacker, to force him into a wider position thereby presenting him with a narrower shooting angle, and as the attacker gathers himself to shoot, the 'keeper offers the attacker fractionally more 'target' inside the 'near post'. If the attacker takes the bait, the goalkeeper only has to move fractionally sideways to eliminate that target. This may cause the attacker to switch to a target inside the 'far post'. A switch takes time and may not allow the attacker to focus his control to be as accurate as he would wish.

In addition, shots across the goal. . . particularly hurried shots. . . tend to be 'pulled' wide of the target.

Fourth, the goalkeeper must 'stand up' for as long as possible to cause the attacker with the ball to make the first move.

Goalkeeping involves a great deal of bluff and counter bluff. Never play poker with goalkeepers. . . at least not for money!

When about to dive at an opponent's feet, the goalkeeper has some crucial questions to answer very quickly.

1. Will the attacker's foot hit the ball before the 'keeper makes his challenge or after? If the former, the goalkeeper's concern will be to spread himself to present the largest possible barrier to the ball while using his hands and arms to make contact with it if he can.

   If the latter, it may pay him to throw himself at his opponent's shooting leg and the ball. At least he may reduce the force of the kick and thereby the likelihood of injury.

2. Is it likely that the goalkeeper will contact the ball with the attacker committed to going through with his kick?

   If so, the 'keeper's instinct tells him to protect the ball by pulling it into his stomach quickly. Where the goalkeeper reaches the ball fractionally before or at the same time as the attacker, it is probable that he will collect the ball close to his face. If the attacker is already swinging his foot at the ball it will pay the 'keeper to use the ball and his arms as protection against the kick. To pull the ball away from the kick will leave the goalkeeper's head dangerously exposed with the attacker committed to kicking in that direction anyway!

3. Is the dive to feet likely to be completed before the attacker's kick begins but while that attacker is still committed to a full run in the direction of the goalkeeper?

   Here, the goalkeeper must not only collect and pull the ball into his stomach, he must, if he can, roll over presenting his back to his opponent while doing so. 'Going to ground' demands courage and cool judgment. The important thing to remember is commitment to attacking the ball.

   If there is full commitment and the goalkeeper can get the whole of one side of his body on the ground quickly the chances of a shot beating that barrier are minimal.

Against the cleverest attackers, a 'thinking' goalkeeper always has a chance. He may be down but he's never out, not least because he can still use his body, legs and hands spread over seven or eight feet to catch, deflect or push away the ball.

Against unthinking attackers a goalkeeper can never be sure what they will do; usually they don't know themselves.

Great goalkeepers are always alert for any chance to stop the ball anyhow with anything, especially when an attacker thinks that a goal is a certainty.

5.4 Distributing The Ball.

A goalkeeper needs the largest range of distribution skills possible, in much the same way and for the same reasons that all outfield players need them. The greater the range of secure distribution techniques, the greater his possibilities for setting up counter attacks quickly and accurately. In modern soccer, counter attack is 'everything' in that without the skill to take advantage of even half chances to attack, a team will find itself facing instant, heavy defense in all parts of the field almost as quickly as it gains possession of the ball.

A goalkeeper has the following basic methods at his disposal. . . or should have.

5.41 Throws
   (a) The baseball throw
   (b) The sling
   (c) The bowl or roll.
   (d) The basketball throw.

5.42 Kicks.
When kicking he should have at his disposal,
   (e) The volley out of hands
   (f) The half volley(drop kick)out of hands, in the air or along the ground
   (g) The dead ball kick (e.g. goal kick) long or short.
   (h) Kicking a moving ball, on the ground or bouncing, first touch.

Recent changes in the Laws of the Game require goalkeepers to involve themselves in 'out of penalty area' play to an increasing extent. In these circumstances, a goalkeeper needs a full range of kicking and passing skills and a decent level of two footedness in the basic techniques of kicking.

All one footed players will be embarrassed at some time or other in their lives but none to more serious effect than a one footed goalkeeper.

5.411 The Baseball Throw.
This is the most natural of all throwing skills, sometimes called the javelin throw. It is most commonly used for quick, accurate throws at target players upwards of twenty yards away in senior soccer.

The first requirement is for a player to be able to hold or balance and control the ball in one hand while throwing.

The throw is a 'sideways on' movement from a wide standing base in which the rear foot is at right angles to the intended direction. It is from the ground 'purchase' of the back foot that throwing power through the legs, hips, back and arms is initiated and in that order.

Having taken the ball back as far as necessary, commonly called the 'wind up', the back foot is used to cause a powerful turn of the hips whereby the side on position is changed to chest on. The arm is still at optimum stretch behind the thrower's head but begins its late and very fast forward movement in sequence. The throwing hand follows through as the bent elbow straightens into the release and the final effort comes from a forward and downward flick of the fingers.

The principle advantage of the throw is that it is direct; it transfers the ball in a straight line from throwing hand down to a receiver's feet.

5.412 The Sling.

The wind up position for the sling is similar to that for the baseball throw but with the feet not so wide apart. There are two slinging methods, the first is over-arm and the second side-arm. The side-arm sling is risky in that deciding on the point of release requires very precise timing which, when it isn't precise, may cause the ball to fly in any direction.

The ball is carried in the curve (the sling) formed by the fingers and the slightly bent wrist and lower forearm. The swing of the arm from beginning to release is as long as possible i.e. the arm is straight. And the slinging action follows through in the direction of the throw for as long as possible after the ball has left the hand. Any tendency to over balance towards the target should not be resisted.

The sling can cover distances as far as most players can kick when used by a strong and fast thrower. The danger however is in the time taken to set up the throw: to 'wind up' and complete the throwing action. Time enough for perceptive, quick moving opponents to read intention and move to intercept while the goalkeeper is unable, often, to change or stop his action.

5.413 The Bowling (Roll) Throw.

Bowling the ball is an underarm skill and to that extent usable only over relatively short distances and where the receiver will be under no pressure whatsoever. Ten to twenty yards is about the distance over which the technique should be used. In some ways it is an underarm sling since the holding position is the same, but the release aims to transfer the ball along the ground without any bounce. Because of the 'sling grip' on the ball it is possible to stop the skill at an advanced stage should circumstances demand it: when an opponent has read the goalkeeper's intention early and is threatening the target player.

5.414 The Basketball (Two handed) Throw.

Occasionally, when an opponent stands in front of the goalkeeper to limit his ability to launch a quick counter attack, the goalkeeper may choose to use a two handed over-arm throw. He employs an action much like that used by outfield players throwing in from the side lines. To evade the restriction attempted by his challenger he may jump to gain enough height to clear any possible interference by his opponent.

General ball handling skills should be part of every goalkeeper's basic practice routines.

5.42 Kicks.
5.421 Volley Kicking
Where the goalkeeper seeks optimum distance he will either volley the ball out of his hands, punt it, or half-volley, drop kick it.

Kicking accurately out of the hands, volleying, is not an easy technique to learn or to execute. Most goalkeepers transfer the ball into one hand briefly before the actual kicking leg begins its swing. The hand supporting the ball is held at a height above ground which will allow for the required elevation when the ball is kicked.

As the kicking leg swings towards contact, the ball is released and either it is allowed to drop a few inches before the strike or it is struck at the moment when it is neither rising or falling.

To facilitate an easy swing and to gain optimum power from a long leg action, the player may lean to one side and towards the intended direction. Care must be taken not to lose balance, certainly not until the ball has left the player's foot.

Optimum power will be derived from,
- a long leg swing,
- the speed at which the foot is moving when it contacts the ball,
- the length of time that the foot is in contact with the ball which can be a good deal longer than most players think. That means that the follow through must be in the direction of the target. Balance ensures the optimum application of kicking force; such over balance as there may be should be forward in the direction of the target.

5.422 Half Volleying.
Many goalkeepers prefer the directional control and easy power which they gain from half volleying and are prepared to concede some of the greater distance available from the volley.

Because the ball is struck only a few inches from the ground, trajectory is lower than for the volley and usually back spin is imparted. A lower trajectory means that target players are able to interpose their bodies between the ball's flight path and opponents relatively easily. Receiving players are much more likely to 'bring down' and control a half volley.

Some players spin the ball backwards by rotating both holding hands upwards and back wards when dropping the ball. This spins the ball backwards to meet the foot as the half volley is struck.

The kicking action is similar to that used by out-field players executing a low drive.

The body is square on to the ball and the knee action from bent to straight occurs late and very quickly. Power comes from foot speed generated by snapping the kicking knee straight from a fully flexed position rather than from the longer leg swing initiated by a powerful hip movement for the volley or the goal kick.

If the knee is allowed to move directly over the ball before it is straightened into the striking action, elevation is eliminated and the result is a half volleyed low drive.

A major consideration in achieving a clean kick is optimum extension of the ankle and its firmness at the moment of impact.

5.423 Clearing Pass-backs.
Kicking the ball when passed back.

Goalkeepers receive more back passes than they have ever done but they are not able to use their hands for those received from outside the penalty area. Passing back is often the choice, sometimes desperate, of an outfield player under considerable pressure from one or more opponents.

Where possible the goalkeeper should kick back along the same line of travel as the pass. The risk of miskicking increases as the angle between the pass back and the chosen line of kick widens. Diagram 17.

Other than for skillful outfield players, kicking across the line of the pass must be avoided where possible.

This produces problems where the goalkeeper is 'one footed'.

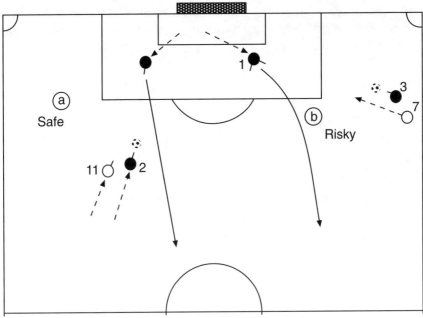

Diagram 17. *(a) narrow angle goalkeeper clearance pass backs (b) wide angle clearance.*

Where the ball is passed back towards the goalkeeper's weak foot, rather than risk an almost certain mis-kick by kicking across the line of the pass, he would be well advised to use his good foot to concede a corner kick or throw in. Where the goalkeeper, in a central position, is receiving a pass towards his weak side but almost directly at him, his choice of kick, having a questionable left foot say, must be with his more reliable right foot and as much down the same line as the pass as possible.

Even in outfield play, too many players deliver passes to their team mates which do not take into account a receiver's dominant or non dominant foot. They just hit their passes towards the receiver leaving him to sort out the reception. Good passers not only allow for a receiver's technical strengths and weaknesses by aiming for his left or his right foot, they take into account what they imagine he intends to do with the ball having received it.

Good soccer players are considerate. They bother to find out what the best interests of their teammates are and service them accordingly.

Where the goalkeeper has to accept a hurried, bouncing pass back from a defender under severe pressure, he may have to stop the ball before kicking clear. Almost certainly he will use his dependable foot to control the ball which with almost equal certainty is likely to drop towards his weaker foot. He should kick clear with his more reliable foot even if the resultant direction is unusual.

Better to be unusual and safe than orthodox and sorry!

To an ever increasing extent, goalkeepers need the skills and the awareness of back players. They must work extra hard, under knowledgeable teachers and coaches, to acquire and improve them.

Chapter 6
Training

Goalkeeping, obviously, is uniquely different from other positions in a soccer team. High level soccer demands considerable 'athletic' ability from out-field players but a goalkeeper performs much more like a gymnast than like a track athlete.

Inadequately trained coaches or teachers, and there are many of them, treat all players the same. Backs, mid-fielders, strikers and goalkeepers all go through the same practice and training routines week in and week out. In intelligently conceived regimes each player, let alone each positional group of players, receives detailed, specialized consideration.

All of the training needs of young soccer players can be accommodated by adapting their skill and technique practice routines which of course involve the use of the ball.

Players under the age of fourteen should be exclusively concerned with improving their individual techniques, their interplay skills and developing their understanding of positional playing principles; the last in exactly the same circumstances as any other player.

These objectives will be achieved through sustained and occasionally intensive practice.

Players rarely need specialized physical training below 12 or 13 years of age and when they do it is almost certain to be remedial. Even so, 90% plus of their preparation will involve technique and skill practice.

Older players, post adolescent, need to compensate for relatively sudden growth and weight increases. This is best achieved through specialized training although skill practices should still take up the major part (75% - 85%) of training and practice time.

To re-iterate, the three 'physical' qualities which, if improved, will enable a goalkeeper to use his techniques and skills more effectively are:

1. Suppleness. . . sometimes called flexibility.
2. Power.
3. Agility.

6.1 Suppleness.
These qualities I defined for my own purposes earlier in the book.

There are any number of gymnastic exercises to be found in good physical training manuals which, undertaken regularly and progressively, will enhance these qualities. A suppling exercise should take a movement to its extreme position and held momentarily, to a count of one to five in thousands. One thousand, two thousand and so on. Gradually over a substantial period of time the extreme position, often called the 'end' position, should be stretched slightly further. The various joint-complexes will move only as much as they are asked to move. If they are never 'asked' to move into extreme positions, they respond by becoming 'lazy'. The older we become, the more our joint complexes do no more than they are asked to do. If we need them to move as far as possible. . . and goalkeepers frequently do. . . we must train them to stretch, bend and twist to meet those needs.

Forgive the repetition, but 'Use it or lose it'.

The earlier that children are trained to be supple, the easier it will be. Achieving and maintaining a full range of movement in all joint complexes should be part of every child's physical education.

It rarely is.

6.2 Soccer Power is:

- the ability to move a resistance at speed or to resist a movement at speed where the movement is that of an opponent.

For a soccer player this means moving his own body weight or the ball (kicking powerfully) or other players (those who challenge him for the ball say).

A goalkeeper needs the power to explode into dives and jumps in all directions. . . forwards, sideways, upwards and backwards. These are gymnastic rather than athletic skills. He also needs the strength and the power to resist the sometimes heavy 'charges' which opponents will use to challenge him for possession of the ball.

6.3 Soccer Agility is:

- the ability to change the position of the body, or its 'shape', at speed.

A goalkeeper not only dives and jumps to catch or punch the ball, he may have to twist in the air and then to roll on landing to regain his feet . . . all while collecting and holding the ball and at speed.

He will certainly have to switch his position in the goal mouth, often very quickly, to face the threat of a strike on goal from different positions.

He will have to run out from goal at speed and then to dive or jump and roll, perhaps to intercept a pass or block a shot at an opponent's feet.

All of these actions require great agility while stretching, bending, twisting and curling, often at optimum speed.

The achievement of increased levels of agility is unlikely without significantly improving suppleness and power.

Power isn't vitally important until a player's weight begins to exceed his strength to handle it. A player in this 'condition' is referred to as having a low power: weight ratio.

The problem may begin, for boys, around eleven or twelve years of age; for girls rather earlier.

The sooner the problem of power: weight ratio shows, the sooner it should be dealt with. . . by sustained, progressive, power-improving exercise.

Keeping weight under control while improving strength is important to goalkeepers. . . and to everyone else for that matter, so my wife says!

6.11 Suppleness Training.

All forms of training or practice should be measurable. Players need to know where they are at any stage in a training program and to what extent they are making progress. The following suppleness training routines are simple tests in themselves.

N.B. It is important that ALL stretching movements are carried out SLOWLY and under full control.

Rhythmical, bouncing movements, e.g. to a strong musical beat, are relatively uncontrolled, by the player that is; they can be dangerous.

Terminology: An exercise or training activity completed once is referred to as one 'rep'.

An exercise completed a given number of times is called a 'set'. e.g. in the following neck exercise, it is recommended that a player completes one set of five reps in each direction a total of twenty times, i.e. four sets of five.

All counts use the word 'thousand' as lasting for one second, e.g. to say, 'one thousand, two thousand, three thousand' takes approximately three seconds.

(a) Neck.
Head Circling
The neck and the point of the chin, stretched in all directions, are used to describe as large a circle as possible. Circle five times in each direction alternately; a total of twenty times each way.

(b) Neck and Head Twisting Sideways.
Keeping the shoulders still, try to touch the point of each shoulder with the point of the chin alternately. Holding each 'end' position for

a count of six (in thousands) rising to eight.
One set of six increasing to one set of ten to each side.

- An 'end' position is the furthest position achieved by stretching a limb or any part of the body which is stretchable.

(c) Head Stretching Forwards and Downwards.

Move and touch the point of the chin as far down the chest as possible. Hold the end position to a count of six thousand rising to eight.
Recover and relax between each 'rep' in a set of eight to ten reps.

(d) Shoulders.

Arm circling slowly upwards and backwards brushing the ears with the fully stretched upper arms on the up-swing each time. Keep the arms parallel as long as possible.
Ten rising to twenty 'reps'.

(e) Shoulders and Back.

Stretch one arm upwards and backwards while stretching the other arm downwards and backwards. Squeeze the arms slowly a little further in each 'end' position, holding the arms there for a count of five.

Ten to twenty 'reps' alternating the positions of the arms each time.

With the arms fully stretched upwards and touching the sides of the head, suppleness will be shown when both arms can be pressed backwards so that the whole of each ear can be clearly seen from the side.

A very high degree of shoulder suppleness will have been achieved when, in the same position, the whole of the head can be seen from the side.

(f) Back.

Kneeling and sitting back on the heels, clasp hands behind the neck. Twist the head and elbows as far as possible to right and to left alternately. Hold each end position for a count of five to eight seconds, recover, relax and repeat.
Ten 'reps', five each way, rising to twenty.

(g) Lower Back.

Standing with one foot forward, clasp hands behind the neck.
With the left foot forward twist the trunk as far as possible to the left,

hold the end position for a count of five to eight seconds.
- Keep both feet flat on the floor all the time.
- Relax and recover facing the front.
- Change feet and repeat in the other direction.
- Try to twist a fraction further in each end position but without strain.

Ten to twenty 'reps' in each direction.

h) Spine, Hips and Shoulders.

Back lying, feet flat on the floor: hands behind the head flat on the floor beneath the shoulders.

Press up on hands and feet into a full back bend. Everything but hands and feet clear of the ground.

Hold the end position for five to eight seconds. Recover relax and repeat ten times.

Back and shoulder strength and suppleness will be seen when the player can produce a high back arch and, without changing the positions of hands or feet, press his knees straight.

(i) Hips.

Wide astride standing, knees straight, lower the trunk as far as possible. Try to touch each knee cap with the forehead. Recover and repeat towards the other knee. Hold the end position for five to eight seconds.

Ten to twenty 'reps' trying to achieve a fractionally lower position each time.

(j) Hips.

Legs wide astride and split forwards and backwards.

Keeping the rear leg straight and the trunk upright, squeeze the hips downwards, as near to the floor as possible.
- Repeat with the legs changed.

Hold each 'end' position to a count of five to eight and repeat with alternate feet forward, twenty 'reps'.

As previously in (e) but twist the trunk to the right when the right foot is forward, to the left when the left foot is forward and so on.

(k) Hurdle sitting, one leg straight in front, the other upper leg fully bent at the knee with the heel tucked in behind.

Keeping both hands off the ground, lower the head towards the front knee and reach forward to touch the toes of the leading foot with the opposite hand, left hand to right foot and so on.

Hold the end position to a count of five to eight, change legs, ten to twenty 'reps'.

The ability to sit with the trunk upright, hands off the ground and achieving a ninety degree angle between the two thighs is a good test of hip suppleness as any high hurdler will agree.

(l) Knees and Ankles.

Sitting upright with both knees together and straight out in front. Keeping the knees straight, raise each leg alternately in turn and circle the ankle clockwise and anti-clockwise slowly and at full stretch. Five times in each direction for twenty 'reps'.

(m) Kneel Sitting,

as in (f), both ankles fully stretched and together take the weight on the hands while 'walking' them backwards into a full back arch.

(n) Ankles.

Running slowly on the spot, stretch the ankle of each foot as it leaves the ground so that the line of the shin through the ankle to the toes is as straight as possible.

Repeat twenty times with each ankle at maximum stretch.

The activities described, if practiced regularly and carried out carefully and steadily even slowly, will significantly improve a goalkeeper's (or for the matter anyone else's) suppleness in all the important joint-complexes.

Suppleness is as important to goalkeepers as it is to gymnasts. It is important to everyone in soccer or outside it.

6.21 Power Training.

Power is the product of weight (mass) and the speed (velocity) at which it can be moved.

A goalkeeper's need for power is similar to that of a gymnast, high jumper or of any athlete who has to move his body position and change its shape at optimum speed.

The goalkeeper's greatest need for power is in leg thrust when taking off one or both feet, with or without a preliminary movement. He also needs fast shoulder and back extension to stretch to catch the ball.

He can improve power in a number of ways.

(a) He can practice goalkeeping movements where the resistance to leg thrust is very low, thereby demanding extra fast muscular work (contraction) to make up for the lack of 'platform' against which he

can push.
This could be in a soft-sand pit or any ground conditions which do not give the player a firm take off platform.

(b) Alternatively he can practice jumping and diving goalkeeping skills while wearing especially heavy boots or a weighted jacket or vest of some kind.

(c) He can combine (a) and (b).

(d) In track and field athletics, the explosive leg power needed in triple, long and high jumping, is enhanced using bounding activities and rebound or 'double jumps'. They are applicable to soccer players needing to improve 'lift off' capabilities.
The essential requirement is the development of instant, optimum speed of 'recoil' when landing from a preceding jump.

Bounding occurs when the running stride is greatly exaggerated into a series of giant strides.
Alternatively a player can use different combinations of powerful hops and steps.
The emphasis must be on the quality of the bounding i.e. the player tries to cover a given distance as fast as possible but with the fewest number of bounds (giant strides).
Bounding may commence with a short running approach to take off from a standing, a single foot or a double foot take-off.

(e) Rebounds.
The player jumps off a platform stool and instantly rebounds over the next obstacle from a two footed take off.
Raising the height of the take off platform or raising the height of the obstacle to be cleared increases the rebound demand and over time will improve explosive elasticity (power) in the legs.

(f) Alternatively, the rebound jump might be to achieve optimum distance rather than optimum height from, say, two successive two footed take-off long jumps.

(g) Successive Double foot 'rebounding' over one, two or three hurdles at appropriate heights, each close to the player's best achievable height, will be effective power training.

The muscular power required to absorb the force of landing and to generate the power necessary to take off for another jump immediately develops elasticity of a kind very important to goalkeepers.

(h) Three preparatory double footed jumps down a long jump run-way towards the take off area or board concludes with a final double-footed jump for maximum distance in the pit.
This will meet the elastic bounding needs of a goalkeeper.

If the starting point is always the same, the player's improvement will be found in the increase in his final landing distance as measured in normal long jump competitions. This activity may become an acceptable regular test of rebound and elasticity power.

(i) Any combination of hops, steps and jumps can be used.
Hopping is particularly strenuous and should not be used by young players or by players who are not in good muscular condition to begin with. That is true for all forms of exercise.

Those out of condition must train in order to train. . . safely that is.

When jumping and rebounding, too many approach steps or jumps and the activity becomes endurance (stamina) biased rather than power developing.
As I have said, training activities carried out on soft sand will be more effective. The player has to work so much harder to achieve explosive reaction to his thrust.
Power training involves short bursts of very intensive work carried out against substantial resistance.

6.31 Agility Power Training.
Soccer agility, as we have seen, is needed to move the whole body into different positions as quickly as circumstances may demand.
For example, as the ball is crossed into the goal mouth, the goalkeeper must hold a goal-line position until he is as sure as he can be of the ball's flight, its speed and where it is likely to land.
He must then time his action. . . which may include a short run, a skip, a change of step, a sideways movement to avoid other players, a jump (or dive) to catch the ball and finally a rolling landing. . . to account for a number of different options.
This is agility. Agility enables the goalkeeper to twist, stretch and curl in the air or to dive and roll on the ground. . . in other words to change the shape of his body, often at great speed.

Those are the elements which agility practices for goalkeepers must include.

Agility training, like training for sprinting, will involve quite short repetitions of training carried out at maximum or near maximum effort with generous recovery intervals between each rep.

One training 'set' will contain up to five or six reps.

Three to five 'sets' of work may be completed in a training session i.e. twenty five work 'reps', plus or minus, interspersed with appropriate rest and recovery intervals. Rest and recovery periods should always involve football activity of some kind, even if carried out leisurely

(a) The goalkeeper starts at the mid-point between the two goal posts, or between two markers eight yards apart representing a goal. Holding a soccer ball and at a signal, the player moves to touch one post completing a forward roll before he does so.

Having touched one post, he moves across, completes a forward roll before touching the other post. Having touched the second post or marker, the goalkeeper runs out to touch the penalty spot or a marker sited twelve yards from goal from where he returns to his starting mark.

The sequence of runs, rolls and recoveries is carried out at top speed. This unit of training is built up into a set and then into a number of sets.

(b) Lying on his back and holding a soccer ball, on a signal the goalkeeper jumps up, runs to a goal post, touches it and jumps to touch the cross bar.

He returns to his starting position on his back. . . the back of his head must touch the ground. . . gets up and runs across the goal to the other post where he repeats the touch and the jump.

The run ends when he is back in his starting position.
3 - 5 repetitions and 3 to 5 sets.

(c) Starting on the mid goal-line point, the goalkeeper runs out of goal to dive onto a ball positioned ten yards from goal and in line with a goal post. As he begins his dive, a player tries to kick the ball as if shooting. The goalkeeper blocks or tries to block the kick, regains his feet and returns to his starting position where after completing a sideways roll he jumps to touch the crossbar.

He repeats the sequence having dived for the ball ten yards from the

second goal post, before returning to his starting position.
Repetitions and sets as for (b).

These agility routines are simple to devise. The activities chosen should include elements of realism. They should not last for longer than 20 seconds and they should include one or two simple gymnastic/athletic movements.

6.4 Planning Personal Training and Practice.

A goalkeeper's training and practice routine must be planned, regular and progressive to a point. It must make increasing demands on those aspects of the goalkeeper's condition which it is designed to improve.

Much like having breakfast or going to work, training routines must become a part of a soccer player's life. He will learn to feel uncomfortable when he has to miss out: so uncomfortable that he doesn't!

Irregular, infrequent practice and training periods are self defeating and a waste of time.

Training sessions will be planned to last from four to six weeks, depending upon the number of sessions in a week. Anything less means that the player is not being given the chance to adapt to and absorb the benefits of the routines.

The effects of training. . . and of skill practice. . . take time before they are revealed in a player's performance.

A training and practice session planned as follows will be useful.

1. Warm-up and Stretching Activity - duration: 15-20 minutes.

Some of the technique practices for two players (one or both being goalkeepers) designed to take place in a ten yard by ten yard square, referred to earlier, will serve as warm-up activities.

When the goalkeeper has raised his body temperature to a condition in which he is beginning to perspire lightly, he should switch to a sequence of suppling (stretching) activities.

2. Technical Practices - duration: 20 -25 minutes.

Against a wall or with another player, the goalkeeper will give special attention to one or two techniques which need to be improved or polished.

'Use it or lose it' highlights the consequences of practice and training especially failing to do it.

3. Rest Interval - duration: 5 minutes.

4. Group tactical skills. 20 +/- minutes.

In this period the goalkeeper practices with his defense on specific aspects of their combined play.

e.g. Line covering when the goalkeeper moves out to catch or punch.
Back defenders clearing the penalty area following a punched clearance. Pass backs from back defenders. . . and so on.

Practice may involve the whole of the defense, eight or nine players, or a defensive unit, the backs say.

Practice may be highly functional and coach controlled or relatively free but 'conditioned' to focus on one or two aspects of group play.

5. Training Activities - duration: 25 minutes.

If the goalkeeper is working on improving his agility, for example, agility work will occupy most of this period of 25 minutes.

Concentrating on one aspect of fitness and doing the work well is better than constantly changing activities thereby reducing the intensity and the effectiveness of the work.

6. Final Activity. 5 minutes +/-.

This is a short period of relaxed activity of any kind during which the player allows his heart rate to return towards normal.

Frequent changes of activity in a program may be more entertaining and enjoyable but they defeat the whole object of the program.
Effective training must involve concentration, achievement, and it has to be seriously hard work.

'No pain, no gain'. There's no easy way to train or practice, even though thousands of players search for one.

A player training program, including skill practice at the different levels, must be carefully prepared long, medium and short term.

(a) Long Term.

The long term plan may cover a playing season, a calendar year or even more than a year if major changes in a player's or a team's playing methods and techniques are envisaged.
Change takes time. The older the players, the longer it takes.

(b) Medium Term.

A medium term plan will take into account the natural divisions into which a year falls. For players at serious levels of commitment and competition, the out of season period. . . the close season. . . and the pre-season period are every bit as important as training 'in' season. The playing season itself falls into 'early' season, 'mid' season and 'late' season phases. These phases will be affected by changes in the attitudes of players, according to the success or otherwise of the team, and also by climatic factors where the climate. . . and consequently playing conditions. . . change significantly.

(c) Short Term.

Finally, short term planning will acknowledge training aims for a unit of playing and training time covering four to six weeks. The training unit will be designed to contribute to medium and long term aims while having the flexibility to accommodate observed needs match to match.

6.41 Long Term.

The full match schedule covering one season, for any leading English Premier Division soccer team is awesome and ridiculous. It will include over sixty highly competitive games, not to mention additional demands made on international players of which a top club will have a large number in its first team squad. It becomes ridiculous when a club extends its schedule to include pre-season and post-season 'friendly' matches. During a season players are persuaded, often, to 'carry' injuries initially of a minor nature which inexorably turn into career limiting chronic conditions.

Money, in soccer, most certainly is the root of all evil.

When planning preparation schedules, the first item to be included in long term plans is the foreseeable program of matches for the coming season including those that are speculative.

Actual match details. . . which team will be the opposition on this date or that. . . are not important at this stage but knowing when the team is scheduled to play and in which competition. . . assuming that a team plays in more than one competition during a season. . . certainly is.

Pre-season and post season 'friendly' matches must be accounted for; often they are anything but friendly.

The long term general aim is to maintain peak condition and preparedness for the complete match program.

The most important item in peak condition is peak enthusiasm.

Peak condition for a soccer player must be optimal rather than. . . as in the case of a track athlete. . . maximal.

Most countries have a national association cup competition and many also have a national league cup competition both of which schedule their finals for the end of season period.

Assuming that all the clubs in a national league aspire to win the league and either or both of the two cup competitions, it is apparent that planning, long term, must start at the end of a season and work back rather than start at the beginning and work forward.

The reason is that surprise success cannot be catered for sensibly whenever it happens. A team which surprisingly finds itself moving towards a league championship and a cup final say, cannot adjust its preparation schedules at the end of a long season and at two weeks' or three weeks' notice. Far better to have planned for success even if it doesn't happen. It is infinitely easier to lower the intensity levels of preparation than it is to raise them, especially over a relatively short period of time. That's worth thinking about and it will not be easy.

6.42 Training Waves.

Thoughtful managers and coaches try to achieve a preparation wave, or rhythm, covering the match-to-match 'week'. Others extend their 'wave' over a period of two weeks, incorporating a minimum of three matches, where the first and last matches are away from home. The idea being that a home match in the middle of a three match schedule can be more easily accommodated as part of a two week training wave than can an away game.

Some professional trainers, faced with the enormous demands of a season totaling in excess of sixty major matches during a thirty-six to forty week period, try to incorporate a series of 'waves' each of which lasts for four to six weeks. These waves incorporate the pre-season and the post season involvement. Some clubs place strict embargoes on the amount of time during which players are totally free from club training and preparation. Players are allowed no more than fourteen days absolute freedom from preparation of any kind during the 'close' season. During the intervening periods they take part in limited but programmed physical activities designed to maintain certain levels of soccer fitness. In my experience most professionals have personally devised activity programs which they follow even during their so-called holidays.

In a six week wave, for example, the first two weeks preparation would be at a fairly high level of intensity, (80%) the third week moderately intensive (60%), the fourth and fifth weeks at peak intensity (90% - 100%). The sixth week would be a recovery week during which preparation momentum would be allowed to work for itself (40%).

In a four week cycle, the first three weeks would be used to move from say a 75% level in week 1, to 85% in week 2 and 90% to 100% in week three with the fourth week used to allow training momentum to take over at say a 50% level.

'Momentum' periods would involve technical and skill practice but at a fairly low level of intensity.

The problem with long, intensive, competitive commitments, as in England for example, is not only the unreasonable physiological demands which a ridiculous playing season makes but the mental slog and grind experienced by even the most enthusiastic players.

Players simply cannot maintain an even peak of playing and training condition. The 'ups and downs' have to be minimized, otherwise players' conditions deteriorate seriously. Players 'over the top' in playing condition are those most likely to suffer injuries both acute and chronic. Regular respite and recovery periods, mental and physical, are absolutely necessary if fatigue is not to become exhaustion; in English soccer it often does.